2

THE GREAT CANADIAN TRIVIA BOOK
2

Mark Kearney and Randy Ray

HOUNSLOW PRESS
A MEMBER OF THE DUNDURN GROUP

Hounslow Press
A Member of the Dundurn Group

Publisher: Anthony Hawke
Editor: Liedewy Hawke
Printer: Transcontinental Printing, Inc.

Canadian Cataloguing in Publication Data

Kearney, Mark, 1955-
   The great Canadian trivia book 2

ISBN 0-88882-197-2

1. Canada — Miscellanea   I. Ray, Randy, 1952-   .   II. Title.

FC61.K43 1998   971'.002   C98-930657-7
F1008.K43 1998

1   2   3   4   5   LH   01   00   99   98   97

THE CANADA COUNCIL | LE CONSEIL DES ARTS
FOR THE ARTS | DU CANADA
SINCE 1957 | DEPUIS 1957

We acknowledge the support of the **Canada Council for the Arts** for our publishing program. We also acknowledge the support of the **Ontario Arts Council** and the **Book Publishing Industry Development Program** of the **Department of Canadian Heritage.**

 Printed on recycled paper.

Hounslow Press
8 Market Street
Suite 200
Toronto, Ontario, Canada
M5E 1M6

Hounslow Press
73 Lime Walk
Headington, Oxford
England
OX3 7AD

Hounslow Press
250 Sonwil Drive
Buffalo, NY
U.S.A. 14225

Contents

2) OUR NATURAL WORLD

3) LET US ENTERTAIN YOU

4) FINANCIAL FACTS AND PECUNIARY
   PECULIARITIES

5) A SPORTS TIME OUT

6) PEOPLE MAKE CANADA TICK — CRAZY CANUCKS? NOT REALLY!

7) MUSIC LOVERS TAKE NOTE

8) OUR POLITICAL AGENDA

9) THIS, THAT, AND THE OTHER THING

Acknowledgements

In preparing our second book of Canadian trivia, we once again drew on the resources and help of many people. As always, we're grateful to the librarians, authors, historians, researchers, academics and other experts who dusted off documents, books, and photographs to help us chase down answers to the many questions posed to them. As for all the photographers and those who supplied us with photos — we appreciate your assistance.

This time around we also want to thank people who suggested questions (and in some cases provided the answers), who tipped us off about some interesting information they'd heard about, or who supported our trivia projects. A special thanks to Bruce Williams, Arthur McCudden, Mike Kennisic, Chip Martin, Dalyce Newby, Nigel James, Brian McAndrew, Marg Munhall, Barbara Blake, Margot Griffin, Robin the lawyer, Jayne Anderson, and the folks at the Sports Hall of Fame, the Hockey Hall of Fame, the Library of Parliament, and the Parliament Hill Information Office.

We'd also like to thank all the radio and TV hosts who eagerly responded to our first book and to the idea of a second one, and to the newspaper and magazine editors and reviewers for their coverage of our trivial pursuits. We're grateful to the bookstore managers and their staff who supported and promoted our first trivia book, especially those who invited us to sign copies in their stores. We hope to see you again soon.

A special appreciation to Tony Hawke, Ian Payton, Kirk Howard, Scott Reid, and all the folks at Dundurn/Hounslow for their enthusiastic support and encouragement of Canadian trivia, and once again to Liedewy Hawke for her keen eye and sharp editing pencil.

Finally, a tip of our hats to readers — those who sent us ideas and information and visited our web site, and who made our first book a Canadian bestseller. It's nice to know we produced a book you found entertaining and educational. We hope you'll find this book as interesting as the first.

Mark Kearney and Randy Ray

Preface

Although some Canadians may not be aware of it, there are so many remarkable things about our country that we just had to do a second trivia book. The more fascinating facts we dug up, the more odd and astonishing items we came across.

Who was the Canadian accused of killing famed escape artist Harry Houdini with a blow to the stomach? Are the streets of Yellowknife really paved with gold? What was Canada's connection to those famous "Paul McCartney is dead" rumours of the late 1960s? *The Great Canadian Trivia Book 2* has all these answers and more.

If you enjoyed reading about Canada's storied past, curious characters, and cultural idiosyncrasies in *The Great Canadian Trivia Book*, then you're in for another treat with this book. And we've provided much more detail this time around for you to savour.

In these pages, you'll discover the Canadian who was responsible for introducing the glove to professional baseball, the story behind Canada's blue two-dollar bill, how the robbery phrase "Hands Up" got its start, the origins of our "national cocktail," why Niagara Falls has run dry more than once, and how long it takes a drop of water to make its way through the Great Lakes.

Think it's impossible for a president of the United States to have been Canadian? That a hockey player could have been charged with murder for an on-ice incident? Or that a Canadian rock group would turn down a chance to play at the famous Woodstock Festival of 1969? *The Great Canadian Trivia Book 2* will have you thinking again. And again.

To Janis and Catherine for listening to, and even encouraging, our trivia ramblings. To Marcus, Andrew, and Christopher Ray, for hearing more talk about Canadian trivia than they ever bargained for. And to Bas and Shirley Kearney, for thinking it was okay that their youngest son wanted to make a living as a writer.

Our Storied Past

What can you say about a country that buried one military hero four times and another legendary figure standing up? Canada may have become a country in a relatively peaceful way, but that doesn't mean we haven't had our share of historical peculiarities along the way.

We trained spies for World War II, had a Victoria Cross winner who didn't even fight in a battle and another VC who was the president of the Toronto Maple Leafs; we welcomed American draft dodgers to Canada in the sixties — the 1860s, that is — and came up with three "last spikes" to hammer into our cross-country railroad.

And let's not forget the American president who just may have been a Canadian.

QUESTION? *Why was Sir Isaac Brock, hero of the War of 1812, buried four times?*

ANSWER. It does seem a bit excessive, doesn't it? Here's the story: When Brock was shot and killed at the Battle of Queenston Heights on October 13, 1812, his body was taken to Government House in what is now Niagara-on-the-Lake, where it lay in state until October 16.

According to the book *Burying General Brock* by Robert Malcomson, Brock was taken from there with great pomp and ceremony and buried in a bastion in the northeast corner of nearby Fort George. His colonial aide-de-camp, Lieutenant Colonel John Macdonell, who was killed in the same battle, was buried with him. A twenty-one-gun salute was fired when the two caskets were lowered in their graves, and Americans at Fort Niagara offered a similar salute. Even though Americans captured Fort George in 1813, the graves remained undisturbed.

The legislature for Upper Canada decided in 1814 that a monument should be erected near Queenston where Brock fell. It took some time to raise money for the monument, and though it wasn't completed yet, Brock's second burial took place there on October 13, 1824. A crowd of about eight thousand were on hand to see Brock and Macdonell's bodies moved from Fort George to the monument ten kilometres away. It was said that as many Americans as Canadians witnessed the event. The monument was never completed to its original design but still stood forty-one metres high with a base six metres square and six metres high.

On April 17, 1840, an explosion shook the tower and severely damaged it. The mastermind behind the explosion was Benjamin Lett, an Irish-Canadian who had been involved in the Rebellion of 1837 and was seeking revenge against the British. He was arrested in the United States on other charges and eventually went to prison.

By 1842, officials decided a second tower should be built, with plans calling for it to be the second tallest structure of its kind in the world, behind a tower honouring the Great Fire of London in 1666. Work began in 1853, and it was necessary to remove the remains of Brock and Macdonell again and place them in temporary graves in a small cemetery in the village of Queenston.

The fourth and final burial took place on October 13, 1853, with about fifteen thousand people attending, including veterans of the War of 1812. Work on the tower continued until 1858, and the structure was officially inaugurated on October 13, 1859.

QUESTION? *Is it true that Gabriel Dumont, commander of the Métis forces during the North-West Rebellion, was buried standing up?*

ANSWER. Legend has it that Dumont was buried vertically in the Batoche cemetery in Saskatchewan on the banks of the South Saskatchewan River. Why? Because it would allow him to see the enemy coming from the river side, author Nancy Miller writes in her book *Once Upon A Tomb: Stories From Canadian Graveyards*.

Another explanation is that he wanted to face the river because it was one thing the white people he despised couldn't change. The grave is marked by a great slab of rock, the biggest individual marker in the cemetery, according to Miller.

The Batoche cemetery was the scene in 1885 of a key battle in the North-West Rebellion, which had been caused by conflicts over land issues. It pitted Métis Leader Louis Riel, Dumont and Métis fighters against 800 to 900 Canadian government soldiers led by Major General Frederick Middleton. The Métis forces were soundly defeated, which effectively ended the rebellion. Plain wooden crosses at Batoche mark a mass grave for the Métis who died in the skirmish.

After the battle Dumont fled to the United States. He died in 1906, after returning to Saskatchewan to resume life as a hunter.

Métis leader Gabriel Dumont is buried standing up.
[NAC/C27663]

QUESTION?

I'm told that Newfoundland entered Confederation on April Fool's Day. Is this another Newfie joke?

ANSWER.

Whoever told you is almost right. Apparently, Newfoundland was scheduled to officially join Canada on April 1, 1949. That date was chosen because it is usually the beginning of the fiscal year for government and most businesses. However, Newfoundland premier, Joey Smallwood, vetoed that date.

He said that after all the work it took to join Canada, he didn't want anyone joking about the new province linking up on April Fool's Day. The official joining was pushed back a few hours and Newfoundland became the tenth province on March 31.

Confederation and April Fool's Day didn't mix for Premier Joey Smallwood.

[NAC/PA117105]

QUESTION?   *Who is Canada's most decorated war hero?*

ANSWER.   Other Canadians, including flamboyant pilot Billy Bishop, have received more medals, but the hero who received the most decorations for gallantry before the enemy (as in U.S. military tradition), is Lieutenant Colonel William Barker. In fact, in his book *Barker VC, William Barker, Canada's Most Decorated War Hero,* author Wayne Ralph describes Barker as "the most decorated hero not just of the First World War but of all our wars."

Gallantry awards won by the prairie farmer's son from Dauphin, Manitoba, are: The Victoria Cross; the Distinguished Service Order and Bar; the Military Cross and Two Bars; the French croix-de-guerre; two Italian Silver Medals for Valour, plus three Mentions-in-Despatches. The Canadian Daily Record of the Overseas Military Forces of Canada once wrote that Barker, "the third Canadian airman to win the VC … holds the record among Canadians for fighting decorations won during the war."

In all, Barker was recognized twelve times for gallantry while flying with Britain's Royal Flying Corps and later with the Royal Air Force. This number of awards probably makes him the most decorated military hero in what was the British Empire.

Barker developed a love for flying while watching demonstration flights at industrial exhibitions in Winnipeg between 1910 and 1914. He won his Victoria Cross on October 27, 1918, for single-handedly taking on between fifteen and thirty German flyers in Fokker D.VII scout planes while piloting a Sopwith Snipe over the Mormal Forest in France. He was credited with destroying four enemy machines but was shot down in the battle and almost died. In total, he had victories over fifty enemy aircraft during his air force career, forty-six while piloting the same aircraft, Sopwith Camel B6313.

At reunions long after the war, Barker's former air force pals remembered him as a "god-like, larger than life warrior," writes

Ralph, a Newfoundlander based in White Rock, British Columbia. Ottawa historian Fred Gaffen, head of publishing at the Canadian War Museum, describes Barker as a "hero and an idol ... a daring type of guy."

Canadian air ace Bishop, a lieutenant colonel who was born in Owen Sound, Ontario, was credited with seventy-two victories and was awarded eight gallantry awards, plus two Mentions-in-Despatches, including the Victoria Cross for his single-handed attack on a German airfield on June 2, 1917. At the end of World War I, Barker had logged more than nine hundred flying hours, Bishop about four hundred. Bishop won another award, the Commander of the Bath, in World War II but it was for his contributions to the war effort, not for gallantry.

After the war, Barker and Bishop ran an aircraft company in Toronto; it had financial difficulties and folded in 1922. Barker joined the Canadian Air Force as wing commander in 1922 and was acting director of the Royal Canadian Air Force when it was created on April 1, 1924. He stayed with the RCAF until 1926, and while he was there he was one of those who were instrumental in having parachutes introduced to both the RCAF and the RAF.

In 1926, with his ambition to head the RCAF stalled, and plagued by post-traumatic stress disorder and physical pain from his combat wounds, he turned to alcohol. He served briefly as president of the Toronto Maple Leafs hockey team, likely in 1927–28, and later was employed as vice-president and general manager of Fairchild Aircraft Limited.

He died on March 12, 1930, at age thirty-five, in a peacetime air crash at Rockcliffe, Royal Canadian Air Force Ottawa Air Station. The tragedy occurred while Barker was demonstrating an open cockpit biplane known as the Fairchild KR-21. The newspapers reported that his state funeral in Toronto on March 15, 1930, was attended by fifty thousand people, and described it as the largest in the city's history up to that date.

William Barker poses with a captured Fokker D.VII aircraft at the Hounslow Aerodrome in London, England in April 1919.

[NAC/PA-006070]

QUESTION?

Is it true that North American Natives did not invent scalping but learned it from white settlers?

ANSWER.

Yes. Although old Hollywood movies would make you think otherwise, the practice of scalping goes back at least 2,500 years to the Scythians of southern Russia. According to the book *Heritage of Canada*, scalping in North America probably began with a governor of the New Netherlands colony who wanted Native people killed. He paid for the scalps, considering them proof of the Natives' death.

By the eighteenth century, apparently, the British were paying for French scalps, and vice-versa, and both paid for Natives' scalps.

Natives took up the practice and in some tribes the taking of scalps became a symbol of warrior status. Scalps were usually taken from the dead, but occasionally people were scalped and still lived. Some people were then allowed to return home as a warning of what could happen.

QUESTION? *I know Canadians fought in the American Civil War, but is it true some fought on the side of the South?*

ANSWER. Almost fifty thousand people from what would become Canada fought in the U.S. Civil War, primarily for the North. In fact, many Canadians were awarded the Congressional Medal of Honor, America's highest military honour, for their participation.

However, as many as two hundred enlisted for the South. Thomas Brooks, author and amateur historian who has researched Canada's involvement in the Civil War extensively, explains that the side on which soldiers fought was often related to where they lived. New Orleans, for example, was a busy port, and many foreigners, including those from what is now Canada, lived there when war broke out.

Others may have drifted to the South to find work and joined up when the war erupted in 1861. In fact, Brooks has written a history of the Tenth Louisiana Infantry, which was called "Lee's Foreign Legion" because soldiers from around the world fought in it.

"Friends of these people were signing up to fight and that certainly is a motivation in any war, that sense of adventure," Brooks says.

One of the more famous Canadians who chose to fight for the South was Dr. Soloman Secord, who was a great-nephew of Laura Secord. He left his home in Kincardine, Ontario, and travelled to Georgia where he enlisted in the Twentieth Georgia Infantry as a surgeon.

There was a touch of irony to this because Secord was known as an abolitionist (that is, he opposed slavery) and, in fact, almost got hanged in Georgia several years before for speaking out against slavery, Brooks points out. But Secord had many friends in Georgia and probably signed up to help these people out.

Secord was captured at Gettysburg on July 5, 1863, became a prisoner of war in Maryland, but escaped in October of that year and joined up with his regiment in Tennessee. He finally resigned his commission in late 1864, and returned to his Kincardine home.

Secord was a highly respected doctor in the community, and when he died in 1910 a monument was erected in his memory. Brooks believes this is the only monument to a Confederate officer in Canada.

Another connection between Canada and the South is that the last acknowledged survivor of Pickett's Charge at the Battle of Gettysburg is buried in Canada. William Hatcher Barnett had come from Virginia to visit his sons, who had immigrated to Alberta, and he died of a heart attack in Bottrell, Alberta, in 1934. He's buried in a small cemetery about fifty miles from Calgary.

QUESTION?

It has often been written that, when John Cabot landed in North America, cod off the coast of Newfoundland were plentiful enough to impede the progress of his ship and could be caught with baskets. Is this true?

ANSWER.

A. In his book *The Cabot Voyages and Bristol Discovery Under Henry VII*, author James A. Williamson makes it clear there was an abundance of fish in the waters of the Atlantic as the Italian explorer approached the shores of Newfoundland in 1497. But whether the fish were so thick that they slowed his ship the *Matthew*, and whether they were cod, is another matter.

Williamson notes that in a letter to the Duke of Milan on December 18, 1497, the Milanese Ambassador to England, Raimondo di Soncino, wrote: "The area is swarming with fish which can be taken not only with baskets but in baskets let down with a stone so that it sinks in the water." Di Soncino also wrote that the fish were so abundant that they could render the English demand for fish independent of Iceland. Other, more recent, writings, including a May 1997 article in the Canadian Airlines in-flight magazine, mention fish were so numerous that they slowed Cabot's ship.

Dr. Leslie Harris, chair of a federal panel which in 1989–90 reviewed the decline of northern cod stocks, dismisses both claims, however, as "exaggerations not uncommon in travellers' tales ... typical examples of hyperbole."

Dr. Harris, a former president of Memorial University in St. John's, Newfoundland, notes that none of those who wrote about the fish seen on Cabot's voyage were on the ship and also that documents of the day weren't definitive about the kind of fish seen by Cabot's crew.

If the fish were cod, it is quite possible they could be brought into a ship in baskets, says Dr. Harris. As a youngster in the 1930s he used to do just that near Placentia Bay on the south coast of Newfoundland. "If you put bait in the basket, in five minutes you could bring up a basket full of cod," he says. "But to dip baskets in the water and fill them with fish, I don't think that was possible [in Cabot's day]."

To impede a ship, Dr. Harris says, cod would have to be "top to bottom" and that simply has never happened. In his opinion, if fish slowed Cabot's boat or were pulled from the sea in copious quantities in baskets, they were likely caplin, a bait fish that even today can fill the seas in some places from top to bottom. "At the right time in June, in spawning season, they do fill the sea from the bottom to the surface, and that could impede a boat ... and there could be some cod mixed in with them," he says.

Caplin are an important commercial fish bought by the Japanese for their eggs.

QUESTION?

What became of the World War II spy camp that was set up in Canada by Sir William Stephenson, also known as A Man Called Intrepid?

ANSWER.

The spy school, known as Camp X, was set up by the British on a 260-acre site straddling what is now the border of Whitby and Oshawa, Ontario, near the shores of Lake Ontario. The British Intelligence Service set up the camp there because they wanted to train Americans in espionage on a site far from their enemies but close to the United States and accessible by water.

The camp was built in 1941 on the former property of a farmer named Sinclair. The camp, officially known as Special Training School 103, housed trainees from all over the world, including, according to some sources, Ian Fleming who later gained fame as the author of the James Bond books. However, David Stafford maintains in his book *Camp X* that there are so many inconsistencies surrounding this claim about Fleming that it is probably a myth. He also writes it's unlikely that Stephenson had been given the code name Intrepid. It is true, however, that Igor Gouzenko, the famous Russian who defected to Canada in 1945, was held at Camp X.

As many as five hundred people were trained at the camp between 1941 and 1944, and it was heavily armed to keep away any curious townsfolk. Although the training ended before World War II was over, Camp X continued as a functioning military installation until the 1960s. The site was sold to the municipalities in the early 1970s and all but one building, which was moved to an animal shelter, were torn down. The cities wanted the land for industrial use.

There is very little evidence these days that the camp existed. However, Intrepid Park in Whitby is a 15.05 acre site on the waterfront that has a small monument identifying the location as Camp X. There are other signs with information about Camp X in the park, as well as two photos. A Liquor Control Board of Ontario warehouse occupies much of the area to the north of the park, on what was formerly Camp X territory.

QUESTION?   *Was there an American president who was born in Canada?*

ANSWER.   According to the U.S constitution, a person can only become president if he or she was born in the United States. That's why controversy surrounded the question whether Chester A. Arthur, the twenty-first president, had the right to the job.

Arthur was officially listed as having been born in Fairfield, Vermont, a town in the northwest corner of the state near the Canadian border. But over the years some people have argued that Arthur was in fact born across the border in Quebec. Actually, *Burke's Presidential Families of the United States of America* states that despite the official birthplace, Arthur "was probably born in Canada." Other sources make the same claim, almost off-handedly, but argue that since his parents were U.S citizens, Arthur's eligibility for the presidency wasn't challenged.

But his eligibility was, in fact, challenged around 1881 when Arthur was the vice-presidential candidate running with James Garfield. Several of Arthur's political enemies spread rumours that he was born in Canada and should be disqualified from the race. According to Thomas C. Reeves, a biographer of Arthur, the Democrats hired a New York attorney named Arthur Hinman to explore these rumours and make a report. Hinman seems to have got carried away because he came back saying that Arthur was born in Ireland and was brought to the United States as a boy of fourteen. Hinman abandoned this theory, however, and later alleged that Arthur was born in Quebec (Lower Canada at the time) at his grandparents' house. According to Hinman, Arthur's mother often visited her parents in Dunham, in Quebec. Hinman published a pamphlet in 1884 called "How A British Subject Became President of the United States."

Another biographer, George Howe, describes this theory as "an interesting hoax" which received little attention at the time. Because many people saw Garfield as a young, vital president, they probably felt they didn't have to worry much about Arthur's background.

In 1881 Garfield was assassinated, however, and Arthur became president. Apparently, one acquaintance was heard to say in disbelief, "Good God, Chet Arthur, president of the United States." Arthur had never held elected office in his life but had been more of a backroom political figure. He had also distinguished himself as a lawyer fighting a case in which he defended a black woman who had been kicked off a streetcar. His victory in that case eventually led to the desegregation of the New York transportation system.

The day after Arthur took the presidential oath, the *New York Sun* ran an article refuting the claim that Arthur was born in Canada.

But there are interesting tidbits surrounding this story. First, several sources list Arthur's birth date as October 5, 1830, but Reeves maintains that Arthur was actually born on October 5, 1829, and changed the date out of vanity. Arthur's father was an Irish immigrant who first came to Canada, living in Stanstead and Dunham, Quebec, and eventually preached in communities in both Quebec and Vermont. Arthur's mother, Malvina, did live in Quebec for a time and her parents lived there until the 1850s. As well, before he died, Arthur destroyed all his personal papers. And while Arthur was listed as being born in Fairfield, some residents believe he was really born in nearby Waterville, Vermont.

Reeve and other scholars dismiss Hinman's claim (as did most of Arthur's contemporaries), but it was certainly an elaborate story. According to Hinman, the Arthurs had three sons, William Chester Alan, who was born in Dunham, Quebec, Chester Abell who was born in Fairfield, and William born in Hinesburgh, Vermont. When the second William was born, William Chester dropped his "William" name and went by Chester Alan (he's the one who became president). He retained the name Chester because his other brother, Chester Abell, had died in infancy and so now the "Chester" name was available. He also appropriated the birth record of this second brother so that he could sustain his American citizenship, Hinman claimed.

And as for why there was no record of this death of the second son, Hinman argued that Arthur's father had sold the body to a medical school. In the end, there seems to be no proof that Arthur was born in Canada, and there is a marker in Vermont pointing out where the twenty-first president was supposedly born. Arthur died on November 18, 1886.

QUESTION?

Who was the first Canadian prime minister to meet with an American president and what happened?

ANSWER.

Sir John A. Macdonald was the first Canadian prime minister who, while in office, met a U.S. president. Macdonald was a member of the British commission that went to Washington in 1871 to discuss trade, especially fishing rights.

Macdonald, though prime minister, was the only Canadian representative on the British negotiating group whose task it was to work out a deal between Canada and the United States. And even then the British appointed Macdonald reluctantly, according to the book *The Presidents and the Prime Ministers* by Lawrence Martin.

Relations between Canada and the United States were dicey at best in those days because the U.S. president, Ulysses S. Grant, firmly believed that Canada should be annexed by the United States. Macdonald and many other Canadians were vehemently opposed to such an idea.

When Macdonald arrived in Washington, he was not officially welcomed by Grant nor by any other U.S. official. During his eleven-day stay in Washington, Macdonald proved to be a lone voice in trying to protect Canada's interests. Neither the British nor the Americans were in favour of the suggestions he made to protect Canada's rights.

Sir John A. Macdonald was the first Canadian prime minister in office to meet with an American president.

[NAC/C2090]

Grant was aloof for most of the visit and only met Macdonald twice, once to be introduced and another time to say goodbye. Macdonald apparently didn't think much of Grant either. James Simeon, a political science professor at York University, asserts that Grant's views on Canada and his desire to take over the then-not-quite-four-year-old country may explain why the American president avoided anything more than a brief encounter with Macdonald.

The first American president to visit Canada while in office, by the way, was Warren G. Harding, who came to Vancouver in the summer of 1923, shortly before he died.

QUESTION?   *Who was the black Canadian who won the Victoria Cross back in 1857?*

ANSWER.   William Hall, a sailor with the Royal Navy, was the first black person and the second Canadian (after Alexander Dunn) to win the Victoria Cross. He won it for "gallant conduct" at the Indian Mutiny of 1857.

Hall was born in Horton Bluff, Nova Scotia, in April 1827, the son of an African slave who had been brought to Nova Scotia by the British. Hall went to sea at age seventeen and joined the Royal Navy in 1852. In 1856, while Hall served in the Crimean War, the Victoria Cross was instituted to reward soldiers for gallant service.

As an Able Seaman, Hall was on the HMS *Shannon* in Hong Kong when a mutiny broke out in India. The rebels held the town of Lucknow, a key area which needed to be recaptured. Sailors from the *Shannon*, including Hall, brought large guns to within twenty yards of the wall of Shah Nejeef, a mosque that had been converted to a fort, and opened fire. The rebels returned their fire and killed all the sailors except Hall and a Lieutenant Young, who kept sending shell after shell into the mosque's wall. Eventually the two survivors created so much damage that the rebels fled, and it was for this brave action that Hall received the medal.

Hall stayed in the navy until 1876 and then returned to farm at Avonport, Nova Scotia, where he died in 1904. He was initially buried in an unmarked grave, but a monument was erected in his honour in 1947 by a branch of the Canadian Legion. In addition to being the first black man to win the Victoria Cross, he was also the only Canadian to win it with a blue ribbon attached. All navy recipients received the Cross with a blue ribbon until 1917, when it was changed to crimson.

QUESTION?

Were draft dodgers who came to Canada to avoid fighting in the Vietnam War the first American draft evaders to settle in Canada?

ANSWER.

No. The concept of dodging the draft began with the Civil War in the 1860s. As a matter of fact, there is a place in New Brunswick, in Carleton County's Mapleton District, that is referred to as Skedaddle Ridge. Many Americans had settled in that area after skedaddling across the border from Maine to escape having to fight in the war.

Americans and people in what is now Canada had been crossing each other's borders for years, often to find work or to settle in a new home. But once the Civil War began and Abraham Lincoln became desperate for soldiers to fight for the North, the border crossings took on a different slant. In addition to offering men money to sign up, the government enacted legislation by 1862 that drafted eligible men into the army. This legislation included a proviso that a draftee could supply a substitute for himself. This is one of the reasons so many Canadians decided to sign up for the war. There was actually a brisk trade in soldiers of fortune in border cities such as Buffalo and Detroit.

But some American draftees decided to put themselves out of reach of the authorities by crossing into Canada, according to the late historian Marcus Lee Hansen. These men were called "skedaddlers." Desertion and draft dodging were especially prevalent in border states such as Maine, New Hampshire, New York, Wisconsin and Minnesota. Because many of these men were experienced farmhands and labour was in short supply in many parts of Canada, they were initially welcomed. They were often glad of the refuge and would work for lower than average pay. By 1864 these skedaddlers were so numerous (some estimates were as high as fifteen thousand) that Canadians were upset that they had to compete for jobs.

When the war ended, many draft dodgers decided to return home, to America, and an amnesty proclamation in May 1865 assured them they wouldn't be punished. Hansen writes that even people who had left the United States for Canada before the war caught the spirit of the time and moved back to the country where they'd been born.

Ironically, during World War I, it was the United States that, until 1917, provided a convenient refuge for Canadians who didn't want to enlist and fight overseas.

QUESTION?

What is the BNA Act and where is it kept?

ANSWER.

The British North America Act is a statute enacted on March 29, 1867, by the British Parliament, providing for Confederation, or the union of the British North American colonies of New Brunswick, Nova Scotia and Canada (Lower and Upper Canada), under the new name Dominion of Canada.

The BNA Act was Canada's written constitution prior to 1982, when it was renamed the Constitution Act, 1867, as part of the movement toward patriation of Canada's constitution. The Act is a pamphlet containing several sheets of fine parchment bound together by a red ribbon at the left edge. The text is printed in black ink, and a number of inscriptions appear throughout, the most significant of these being the royal assent granted by Queen Victoria on March 29, 1867.

A spokesman for the National Archives of Canada in Ottawa says there are two copies of the BNA Act. One is kept in the Tower of London and the other copy belongs to the British Public Record Office. The latter was borrowed by the Senate of Canada for an exhibition held in the entrance to the Senate Chamber at Parliament Hill, to mark the 125th anniversary of Confederation in 1992.

QUESTION?

What is the story behind the soldier who was awarded a Victoria Cross for action in Canada that didn't involve a battle?

ANSWER.

Timothy O'Hea was born in Ireland and served in the Rifle Brigade when he did something that merited receiving the Victoria Cross. He is the only soldier to have been awarded the prestigious medal for action in Canada and just one of a few that received it without having to face the enemy.

O'Hea won his medal for the bravery he showed on June 9, 1866, when he helped put out a fire in a railway car carrying ammunition. The car burst into flames while stopped at Danville Station, Quebec, and was then disconnected from the rest of the train. O'Hea snatched the keys to the burning car from the sergeant in charge, opened it up, and called for water and a ladder to keep the blaze under control. Because of his quick reaction, the fire was suppressed and damage kept to a minimum.

Several letters were exchanged between the General Officer Commanding the Troops in Canada and the War Office in Britain before it was decided O'Hea deserved the Victoria Cross, the highest honour given to soldiers in what was then the British Empire.

The medal had been introduced a decade earlier, but the provision that an act of bravery take place in the presence of the enemy was suspended between 1858 and 1881. In that time period, a few other soldiers received Victoria Crosses for bravery that didn't involve confronting the enemy, but O'Hea's feat was the only one that took place in Canada.

O'Hea later returned to Ireland, gave the medal to a friend to keep and then went prospecting in Queensland, Australia, where he died in 1874. The medal resurfaced in Australia in 1985.

QUESTION?

How many French Canadians served in the armed forces in World War II? And how many before conscription came into effect in 1944?

ANSWER.

This sounds like a question with political overtones, and unfortunately (or perhaps fortunately) there is no clear answer. Fred Gaffen, head of publishing at the Canadian War Museum, maintains that the question is impossible to answer because there is no clear definition in military records of what is a French Canadian.

Is it someone from Quebec, or is it someone with a French-sounding name or someone who speaks French but happens to live in Ontario, Gaffen asks. The military didn't break down its records into French and non-French Canadian categories, he explains.

Gaffen admits there was a general feeling in Canada that the French didn't sign up for military service as readily as the rest of the country, "but there's absolutely no way to prove it." There were demonstrations against conscription in Quebec (and elsewhere) and a split among English and French politicians about the issue, but there is no evidence to suggest French Canadians took part in the war any more or less than any other group.

When conscription finally came into force by the end of 1944, only a few thousand soldiers were affected and saw front line action, before the war ended in 1945.

QUESTION?   *Did the sister of the last czar of Russia live in Canada?*

ANSWER.   Yes. Grand Duchess Olga Alexandrova spent the last twelve years of her life, until her death in 1960, in a couple of locations in and around Toronto.

The grand duchess, whose brother was Czar Nicholas II, was born in St. Petersburg on June 14, 1882. She was the youngest daughter of Czar Alexander III.

Like all of Russian royalty, she lived the imperial lifestyle during the years leading up to the First World War and became the favourite aunt and confidante of Czar Nicholas's daughters. Her first marriage, in 1901, to Prince Peter of Oldenburg was arranged by the family.

The marriage was annulled in 1916 so she could marry Col. Nikolai Kulikovsky (also spelled Koulikovsky) and she became a nurse. Because she was away in Kiev tending to the wounded, she managed to escape the fate of the many Russian royals who were killed after the Russian Revolution.

She and her husband had a narrow escape when they were arrested by Communist troops in the Crimea. Two bureaucrats argued for so long about the manner in which the grand duchess and her husband should be executed that they managed to get away, and they were later saved by German soldiers who invaded the area.

From the Crimea, Olga, her husband and Olga's mother eventually made their way to Denmark, where they lived in exile. Olga's older sister Xenia later joined them but moved to England some years afterward. The grand duchess and her husband had two children and lived peacefully in Denmark, even after the Nazis occupied that country in 1941. Later, however, Communists in Russia accused her of subversive activities, and it was decided that she move elsewhere. A friend of King George V of England, who was a relative of the grand duchess, made arrangements for her and her family to move to

Canada. They came here in 1948 and settled on a two-hundred-acre farm between Milton and Guelph.

"I immediately felt at home in Canada," she once said. "The vast open spaces reminded me of Russia."

When her husband became too ill to run the farm, they moved to a cottage in Cooksville (now Mississauga). Olga gained some renown as a painter and had a showing of her work in Toronto in the 1950s. During the last months of her life, she lived in east Toronto with another Russian family, the Martemianovs. She died there on November 24, 1960, at seventy-eight years of age (shortly after her sister Xenia, who had died that summer). The grand duchess is buried with her husband in York Cemetery, in Toronto's north end. The newspapers described her death as the end of Imperial Russia.

QUESTION?

Is it true that more than one spike was involved in the ceremony celebrating the completion of the Canadian Pacific Railway? Where are these spikes today?

 ANSWER.

You've hit the nail right on the head. Technically, there were three spikes that played a role in the proceedings at Craigellachie, British Columbia, on November 7, 1885, when railway officials and workers gathered to mark the end of the massive railway-building project.

As we told you in our first *Great Canadian Trivia Book*, a silver spike was made for the ceremony but was never used. There were also two iron spikes. The first was bent when Donald Smith, a.k.a. Lord Strathcona, attempted to drive it into the railway tie; the second was driven into the tie but didn't stay in place very long.

First, the bent spike: It was retrieved as a souvenir by Smith. He had a portion of it shaved off and ringed with diamonds as a gift for his wife Bella, Canadian author Donna McDonald says in her book *Lord Strathcona, A Biography of Donald Alexander Smith*. But in his book *The Last Spike*, author Pierre Berton reports that a number of women — all wives of men who attended the ceremony — were recipients of the jewelry Smith had made. And when several other ladies complained they did not receive souvenirs, Smith had another spike cut up for similar souvenirs, writes Berton.

Second, the spike that went into the railway tie: Once the dignitaries left, it was removed by CPR roadmaster Frank Brothers, who was afraid souvenir hunters would tear up his track. It was later presented to Edward Beatty, then president of the CPR.

So where are these spikes today?

The original last spike — the one that was bent — is at the National Museum of Science and Technology in Ottawa, says David Monaghan, the museum's curator of land transportation. Between four and five inches long, it's cracked and clearly shows where Lord Strathcona had pieces shaved away for jewelry. The spike is occasionally on display and has been lent to other museums. It was donated to the museum in 1985 by descendants of Lord Strathcona in honour of the CPR's centenary celebrations.

The silver spike was mounted on a marble base to be used as a paperweight and is in Toronto, owned by descendants of the family of Cornelius Van Horne, president of the CPR and general manager of the railway during its construction.

To this day, no one knows where the spike that was driven into the railway tie and presented to Edward Beatty ended up. Monaghan has heard rumours that it is owned by someone in the Yukon Territory.

QUESTION?

Who closed the doors that saved the Library of Parliament from the fire that destroyed the rest of the Parliament Buildings?

ANSWER.

Credit for saving the library goes to M.C. MacCormac, a library clerk who was on duty when the fire broke out between 8 P.M. and 9 P.M. on February 3, 1916. Not only did his quick action save the library, it probably saved the lives of several members of Parliament who were in the library.

"Mr. MacCormac, who was present at the outbreak of the fire, promptly had the iron doors leading into the corridor closed against the on-rush of smoke and flames," General Librarian A. D. DeCelles and Martin J. Griffin, Parliamentary Librarian, wrote in a post-fire report to the Parliament led by Prime Minister Robert Borden. "He was probably instrumental in saving the lives of some members who were in the library by refusing to open the doors and by sending them

The Parliamentary Library: Saved from flames by a quick-thinking clerk.
[NAC/PA12381]

safely through the side door, usually kept locked and bolted since the police took charge of the buildings."

Not everyone was so lucky, however. The fire, which started in a reading room and was fueled by piles of newspapers and by varnished wood panels in rooms and corridors, claimed the lives of seven people. Those killed were: Randolph Fanning, an employee at the Parliament Hill post office; Bowman B. Law, M.P. for Yarmouth, Nova Scotia; Alphonse Desjardins, a steamfitter for the Department of Public Works; J. B. René Laplante, Deputy Clerk of the House of Commons; A. Desjardins, a constable with the Dominion Police Force; and Florence Bray and Mable Morin, who were visiting the wife of Albert Sévigny, Speaker of the House of Commons at the time of the fire.

QUESTION?

Where did Canada's early Parliament meet, and what cities were considered before Ottawa won out as the country's capital?

ANSWER.

Before Ottawa became the nation's capital, Canada's parliamentary business was a bit of a travelling road show. During the French regime, Quebec City served as the capital of France's colonies in mainland North America and it kept that status after the surrender of the colony to Britain in 1763. But as English people began moving into the Great Lakes region, consequently demanding a voice in government, it became apparent that Quebec City was too far away. In 1791, the British Parliament passed a bill that split Quebec into Upper and Lower Canada in order to give some political autonomy to the United Empire Loyalists who had opted to live under British rule.

Quebec City remained Lower Canada's capital, and Upper Canada's first capital became Niagara-on-the-Lake, where the first Parliament of Upper Canada met on November 17, 1792. However, the British soon deemed Niagara-on-the-Lake unsatisfactory because it was too close to the United States and also because it was too small a village; most settlers passed it by to put down roots in southwestern and central Ontario. So, the provincial capital was moved to Toronto where it remained until 1840, when the British decided to re-unite the provinces of Upper and Lower Canada following the Rebellions of 1837.

Between 1841 and 1867, the Province of Canada was served by a wandering Parliament, with its business being conducted in Kingston, Montreal, Quebec City and Toronto. But moving the legislature proved to be unwieldy, because each time Parliament changed cities, its records, library and furniture had to be packed up and shipped to the next location, politicians and administrators had to find new lodgings and there was little sense of political continuity.

Eventually, the choice of a location for the permanent capital became a hotly debated topic. French Canadians wanted either Montreal or Quebec to be the capital while the Liberals in Canada West preferred

Toronto or Kingston. In 1857, the question was referred to Queen Victoria. Cities vying for the honour were Kingston, Montreal, Quebec City and Toronto. Bytown, a lumber town which was later renamed Ottawa, won out, however, after Sir Edmund and Lady Head, friends of the Queen, visited the town and lobbied for it. The legislature at first rejected this choice, but eventually Ottawa came to be accepted as the nation's capital.

On September 1, 1860, the Prince of Wales, later Edward VII, laid the cornerstone for the centre block. Less than seven years later, on July 1, 1867, Confederation was a reality, and the Parliament Buildings, with the exception of the Library of Parliament, were completed and ready for the new government.

QUESTION?   *Was a Canadian a key figure in the famous Great Escape of World War II?*

ANSWER.   Although he wasn't in charge of the endeavour, Wally Floody, who surveyed, designed, and engineered the tunnel used by Allied soldiers to get out of the German prisoner-of-war camp Stalag Luft 3, has been called "the architect of The Great Escape."

Clarke Wallace Floody was born in Chatham, Ontario and as a young adult entered the mining industry that was flourishing in Kirkland Lake, Ontario. When World War II broke out, he became a pilot officer in the RCAF's 401 Squadron. A month later he had to bail out of his plane and was captured by the Germans.

As anyone knows who has seen the movie *The Great Escape*, which was based on this famous World War II incident, there were three tunnels built as possible escape routes, nicknamed Tom, Dick and Harry. According to his obituary, Floody was the man credited with overseeing their construction at the camp. In fact, he was considered so vital to the tunnel construction that his senior officers forbade him to join an earlier escape from the camp. He was almost killed twice during the digging of the tunnels, and it was his knowledge gained from the mines of Kirkland Lake that enabled him and others to build the tunnels so well.

"Harry" was the tunnel the soldiers eventually used for the escape. It was 336 feet long and 30 feet underground, which many experts consider a considerable feat given the tools and materials available to the prisoners of war.

Ironically, Floody did not get a chance to use the tunnel because he was moved to another nearby prison camp before the Great Escape took place.

After the war, Floody gave evidence at the Nuremberg Trials, and he later built up and sold many small business enterprises. He died in 1989.

QUESTION?   *In what years were Canada's provinces and territories created?*

 ANSWER. The original country of Canada, known as the Dominion of Canada, was composed of the provinces of Ontario, Quebec, Nova Scotia and New Brunswick. They were united under the provisions of The British North America Act, which was originally known as "An Act for the Union of Canada, Nova Scotia and New Brunswick, and the government thereof, and for the purposes connected therewith."

In 1870, the northerly region, known under various names, including "Rupert's Land," "the Hudson Bay Territory" and the "North-West Territory," was purchased from Great Britain and the Hudson's Bay Company and added to the Dominion, and on July 15, 1870, the Northwest Territories entered Confederation. A large portion of the territory was set aside to form the province of Manitoba, which was also admitted to Confederation on July 15, 1870.

British Columbia joined on July 20, 1871, followed by Prince Edward Island on July 1, 1873. The Yukon Territory, formerly a part of the Northwest Territories, entered on June 13, 1898. The provinces of Alberta and Saskatchewan were formed from the provisional districts of Alberta, Athabaska, Assiniboia and Saskatchewan and were admitted to the Union of Provinces on September 1, 1905. In 1912 a bill was passed to extend the areas of Manitoba, Ontario and Quebec northward by adding portions of the Northwest Territories to each province. The final block of the Canadian federation fell into place on March 31, 1949, when Newfoundland entered Confederation.

QUESTION?

Is it true that many towns and cities in Canada are named after people who helped build the railways that linked the communities together in the early 1900s?

ANSWER.

Canada's railways were gigantic creative forces, often determining where towns would be built and how far apart they would be, notes Ottawa historian Hugh Halliday. And in the process, the names of railway company presidents, officials, stockholders and even construction workers were attached to scores of towns, he informs us.

For example, Melville, Saskatchewan, was named for Charles Melville Hayes, the dynamic president of the Grand Trunk, which opened up a new transcontinental route across the Prairies between 1900 and 1915. Hayes died in 1912, when the Titanic sunk off the east coast of Canada. Another transcontinental line was built by the Canadian Northern Railway. The company pinned a shortened version of its name on the Saskatchewan town of Canora.

The Canadian Pacific Railway did its part as well. Estevan, Saskatchewan, was derived from a combination of the names of Sir George Stephen, president of the CPR when the town was named, and Sir William Cornelius Van Horne, then the railway's chief engineer.

Stephen and Donald Smith (later Lord Strathcona) were born in Banffshire, Scotland, and gave Banff its name. Van Horne was a patron of the arts and selected the town of Holbein, Saskatchewan, to commemorate a famous German painter.

Even relatively insignificant personalities had towns and sidings named after them, according to Halliday. Olds, Alberta, was designated as such for George Olds, a CPR traffic manager and Hornepayne, Ontario, is named after R. M. Hornepayne, financial representative for the Canadian National Railway in London in 1920.

Our
Natural
World

Quick question: how long does it take a drop of water to travel from Lake Superior to the Atlantic Ocean? And how is it possible that Lake Superior isn't the biggest lake in Canada? And just where is the coldest spot in Canada?

If those questions have you scratching your head, put your pencils down and get a little lesson in Canadian geography — trivia style.

QUESTION?　　　　*Has Niagara Falls ever run dry?*

ANSWER.　To many it's unthinkable, but yes, it has happened on several occasions at the hands of Mother Nature, and once when man intervened.

The first and only time both the American falls and the Horseshoe Falls on the Canadian side fell silent was on the night of March 29, 1848, when an ice jam formed on Lake Erie near Buffalo, blocking the water that normally flows along the Niagara River and over the falls, according to Dave Phillips of Environment Canada.

By the next morning a throng of up to five thousand sightseers had converged on the area to find the American falls had slowed to a trickle and the thundering Canadian falls were stilled, Phillips wrote in a book entitled *The Day Niagara Falls Ran Dry, Canadian Weather Facts and Trivia*. Some daredevils explored cavities at the bottom of the dry river, where they picked up bayonets, muskets, swords, gun barrels, tomahawks and other relics of the War of 1812. Others crossed the river above and below the falls on foot, horseback or by horse and buggy — a historic opportunity, to be sure.

But the waterless river course wasn't seen as an opportunity by everyone: Superstitious people became fearful and many went to special church services.

The falls wouldn't stay silent for long, though. On the night of March 31 — thirty hours after Mother Nature turned off the tap — balmy weather and shifting winds dislodged the ice and a sudden wall of water surged down the riverbed and over the falls, restoring the ever-present Niagara spray and rumble and boom of the falls.

The American falls were shut off on six other recorded occasions including in 1909, 1936 and 1947; each time it was because they had frozen over completely. And in 1969 the American side was silent again — this time at the hands of humans. For seven months the U.S. falls were turned off, after the United States Army Corps of Engineers diverted the river to permit repairs to the falls' eroding face.

Phillips believes that Canada's Horseshoe Falls aren't likely to be blocked by ice again. Every winter since 1964 a boom has been positioned at the head of the Niagara River to prevent the formation of ice blockages and to safeguard hydroelectric installations.

QUESTION?

How long does it take for water to pass through the Great Lakes to the Atlantic Ocean?

ANSWER.

If a drop of water could talk, what a story it would tell.

On average, a drop of water which finds its way into Lake Superior from runoff or rainfall takes more than two centuries to travel through the Great Lakes system and along the St. Lawrence River to the ocean, according to Environment Canada's Ontario region office in Burlington, Ontario. To be precise, water that entered Superior in 1794 — the year the Reign of Terror came to an end in France following the French Revolution — didn't make it to the Atlantic until 1998.

The travelling time is based on retention times, or how long, on average, it takes for each of the lakes to replace its water with new water.

By the time a drop of water has passed through Lake Erie, it's been travelling for about 194 years.

[Photo: Mark Kearney]

To get a grip on this theory, think of each of the lakes as a ten-gallon bathtub with the drain slightly open and the tap running slowly. If one gallon of water flows in and another out every minute, after ten minutes you will have emptied ten gallons and added ten new gallons. One drop might come in through the tap and go out the drain in only a few seconds, while another drop might stay in the tub for an hour or more, but the average length of stay is ten minutes.

In Lake Superior, the tap is rain and runoff and the drain is the St. Marys River, which flows into Lake Huron. After 173 years, much of the water in Superior has flowed out of the lake and been replaced with new water. In Lake Huron replacement averages 21 years; Lake Erie, 2.7 years and Lake Ontario, 7.5 years. Add the numbers together and you will see that drops of water which fell into Lake Superior in 1794 flowed into the Atlantic a little more than 204 years later.

The time span is much less for lakes closer to the Atlantic. Water you were swimming in at the beaches of Grand Bend on Lake Huron in 1967, when Canadians were celebrating Canada's one-hundredth birthday, also flows into the Atlantic in 1998, while water which had poured into Lake Erie in 1988, when the Canada–U.S. Free Trade Agreement was signed, also arrives at the ocean in 1998. If your son or daughter is seven and a half years old, water now streaming into the Atlantic was in Lake Ontario at about the same time he or she was born.

It should be noted that not all of the water in each of the Great Lakes is at some point replaced. For instance, 37 per cent of the water that was in Lake Superior 173 years ago is still there, explains Environment Canada.

QUESTION?

While visiting the Channel Islands, I noticed in Guernsey a lot of signs with the word Sarnia. Is there any relationship between Guernsey and Sarnia, Ontario?

ANSWER.

Although historians have different opinions on the subject, there is a theory that the island of Guernsey, which lies off the northwest coast of France, was given the name "Sarnia" by the ancient Romans. What is not in dispute is that Thomas Colborne, a founder of Sarnia, Ontario, gave the city in southwestern Ontario that name because it reminded him of his home in Guernsey.

Several companies in Guernsey have borne the Sarnia name, such as Sarnian Sports and Sarnia Real Estate. The island's anthem is called "Sarnia Cherie." Although most of Guernsey's inhabitants believe that Sarnia is their island's correct ancient name, some historians think that the name the Romans used for this part of the Channel Islands was Lesia.

The other famous connection between Guernsey and Ontario is that Sir Isaac Brock, who fought and died in the Battle of Queenston Heights during the War of 1812, was from Guernsey.

Shops on the island of Guernsey still carry the Sarnia name.
[Photo: Mark Kearney]

QUESTION?   *Is it true that Lake Superior isn't the largest lake in Canada?*

 ANSWER.   It sounds as if we're being tossed a curve here, like the kind our Grade Nine geography teacher used to throw. Lake Superior, with its 82,107 square kilometres of water surface, is easily the biggest fresh-water body in the world. But you have to remember that only part of the lake is in Canada and the rest is in the United States. Only 28,749 square kilometres of Lake Superior are inside Canada, so technically it isn't the largest lake "in" Canada.

The biggest lake entirely encompassed by Canadian soil is Great Bear Lake in the Northwest Territories, which has all of its 31,328 square kilometres within the boundaries of Canada.

In the "solely within Canada" class, number two is Great Slave Lake, also in the Territories. Its area is 28,570 square kilometres.

QUESTION?   *Where in Canada is the North Magnetic Pole located?*

ANSWER.   Because the pole moves at a rate of about ten to fifteen kilometres a year, we can't say exactly where it is as you read this. But when we checked with the Earth Sciences Department of the University of Western Ontario and other sources, the North Magnetic Pole was located on a southwest portion of Ellef Ringnes Island. This is in the Queen Elizabeth Islands, in the Arctic, at approximately 79 degrees north latitude and 104 degrees west longitude. To give you an idea of how far up that is, it's about three thousand kilometres north of Winnipeg.

When the Magnetic Pole was discovered in 1831 by James Clark Ross, it was located on King William Island. Roald Amundsen studied the pole during his 1903 expedition, and shortly after World War II the pole had moved some 250 kilometres northwest to Prince of Wales Island. It reached Bathurst Island by the early 1960s and has been moving northwest ever since. There are several factors that account for its movement, including convection currents in the earth's core. As well, the pole moves during any given day because the sun constantly emits charged particles which eventually cause electric currents to be produced in the upper atmosphere of Earth.

According to information from the Canadian government, the pole is used as a tool for magnetic cartography. Knowing the angle between true north and magnetic north helps in navigation, and maps showing this "magnetic declination" are published every five years.

QUESTION?   *Is there any city or town in Canada that lies on the border of two provinces?*

ANSWER.   Lloydminster is located on the Saskatchewan–Alberta border, 300 kilometres west of Prince Albert, Saskatchewan, and 235 kilometres east of Edmonton. When Alberta and Saskatchewan were created in 1905, Lloydminster, which was originally named Britannia Settlement, found itself divided between the two provinces.

The problem was solved in 1930, when the Saskatchewan town of Lloydminster and the Alberta village of the same name were amalgamated as the town of Lloydminster by order-in-council in both provinces. The town became the tenth city of both provinces in 1958, when it was raised to city status.

QUESTION?

I know Toronto and Montreal are Canada's largest cities, but how do they rank in population compared to cities in the United States and the rest of the world?

ANSWER.

Population figures can vary from source to source, and the way they're gathered can vary from country to country, partly because census data can be taken in different years. Toronto, however, with a listed population of 3.29 million, is smaller in population than six cities in the United States, as the *Information Please Almanac* (49th edition) points out. It ranks just behind metropolitan Miami, while Montreal, with a population of 2.99 million, comes next, just ahead of Detroit. Oddly enough, the figures given for Detroit also include Windsor, Ontario. Shortly after Toronto became a "mega-city" in 1998, however, a newspaper report claimed the city was only smaller than four others in the United States.

The *Almanac* states its editors rank population after consulting detailed maps of each city in conjunction with the most recent official population statistics. It also notes, however, that political and administrative boundaries are disregarded, hence the grouping of Windsor with Detroit.

The U.S cities with higher populations than the two Canadian ones, according to the *Almanac,* are listed, in order, as New York City, Los Angeles, Chicago, San Francisco, Philadelphia, and Miami. As for world rankings, Toronto ranks sixty-fifth, just behind Casablanca, Morocco, and ahead of Ankara, Turkey. Montreal is seventy-second, behind Berlin, Germany, and ahead of Poona, India. The world's largest city is Tokyo–Yokohama with a population of 28.44 million.

QUESTION?   *Is there a Prince Edward Island other than the Canadian province?*

ANSWER.

You might think that such a common name would be in abundance around the world, but it appears there is only one other such island. And it's so obscure that few Gazetteers even mention it. There is, however, a small subantarctic islet about twelve hundred miles southeast of Capetown, South Africa, known as Prince Edward Island. It's a circular island about five miles in diameter that combines with nearby Marion Island, which is thirteen miles long and eight miles wide, to make up what is known as the Prince Edward Islands.

The islands were discovered in the late eighteenth century by explorer Marion du Fresne, who named them Les îles Froides, or "cold islands." Captain Cook later sailed by them on one of his voyages. The islands were formally annexed by South Africa in 1947, and there was, and may still be, a meteorological station on Marion Island.

By the way, our own Prince Edward Island, which is 5,660 square kilometres, was originally named Île St-Jean. It was renamed in 1799 in honour of Prince Edward Augustus, the Duke of Kent and fourth son of George III.

QUESTION?

Where were the first dinosaur remains found in Canada? How old are they and where are they now?

ANSWER.

Many Canadians think the only dinosaur bones unearthed in Canada were found in Alberta and Saskatchewan, but that's not the case.

Richard Day, spokesman for the Canadian Museum of Nature in Ottawa, points out that the oldest dinosaur remains in Canada were embedded in sediments along the Bay of Fundy in Nova Scotia's Minas Basin and are approximately 200 million years old. Evidence of dinosaurs, both foot imprints and isolated bones between 65 and 150 million years old, has also been uncovered in British Columbia; in the northern Yukon Territory; the McKenzie Mountains of the Northwest Territories and on Bylot Island in the Arctic.

But let's not take any credit away from Saskatchewan and Alberta: Day says the dinosaur faunas in the two provinces are among the richest in the world for the Upper Cretaceous period (65 to 75 million years ago), especially those found in the badlands along the Red Deer River at what is now called Dinosaur Provincial Park in Alberta.

The first evidence of dinosaur bones in Canada was found in southern Saskatchewan, when isolated bones of duck-billed dinosaurs, known as hadrosaurs, were discovered, in 1874, by Geological Survey of Canada geologist George M. Dawson, in the Frenchman Formation exposures near Wood Mountain. These bones are believed to be about 65 million years old. Later in the same year, Dawson and his geological mapping party found more evidence, on the Milk River in Alberta, of the duck-billed dinos and these fragments are about 75 million years old.

Other dinosaur remains, generally pieces of leg bones and the vertebral column of hadrosaurs, were found between 1874 and 1884 when J. B. Tyrrell — namesake of the Royal Tyrrell Museum in Drumheller, Alberta — was mapping the area around the Red Deer River near Drumheller for its geological resource potential. Tyrrell found the first dinosaur skull in Canada, from a small tyrannosaurid that was subsequently named Albertosaurus. This 70-million-year-old specimen, discovered at Kneehill Creek, was the first example of the genus found anywhere in the world and is now part of the Canadian Museum of Nature collection. It is not on display.

The first fairly complete dinosaur specimen to be mounted in a Canadian museum was that of a 70-million-year-old hadrosaurian dinosaur, Edmontosaurus, which was collected in 1912 by the first professional dinosaur hunters in Canada, Charles Hazelius Sternberg and his three sons, Charles M., Levi and George, of Kansas. The Edmontosaurus has been on display since 1913 at the Canadian Museum of Nature.

Other dinosaurs can be seen at the Royal Tyrrell Museum, which, with thirty-five complete skeletons on display, has the largest number assembled under one roof in the world. The Royal Ontario Museum in Toronto and the Royal Saskatchewan Museum in Regina also exhibit dinosaur skeletons.

QUESTION?   *Where is the coldest spot in Canada, and is it ever too cold to snow?*

ANSWER.   Even hardy Canucks, who are used to winter, may shiver when they hear that the lowest recorded temperature in Canada (and North America) was -63° C (or -81° F). It froze its way into the record books on February 3, 1947, at Snag, in the Yukon Territory.

But not everyone agrees with climatologists' assessment of this frigid milestone, notes Dave Phillips of Environment Canada. Although Snag is the officially recognized record, people in Mayo, Yukon Territory, believe they were as cold or colder than Snag. They claim they also reached -63° C and have a photograph of the thermometer that shows it. Unfortunately, the records they kept on this were lost in a fire, so Environment Canada can't technically recognize the claim.

Snag at the time was essentially an airport strip where a few people worked, while Mayo is an actual community where people live. Citizens there believe they can lay claim to being Canada's coldest inhabited spot. Today, Snag is merely an abandoned airstrip where no one lives or works.

The Ontario community of White River, north of Lake Superior, advertises itself as "The Coldest Spot in Canada," but that's a myth, says Phillips. Even with its claim of a recorded temperature of -72° F, it still can't match Snag or several other communities in Canada.

And no matter how cold it gets in the far north, it can still snow. Environment Canada explains that to produce snow the air must hold at least some moisture in gaseous form. The water vapour must be cooled beyond the freezing point, at which snow crystals form.

Because warm air holds more moisture than colder air, the heaviest snowfalls and largest flakes occur at temperatures close to freezing. As the air becomes colder, the flakes become finer and finer. It is never too cold to snow, but the colder it is the less snowfall there will be.

If that's any consolation.

QUESTION?   *What is the southernmost point in Canada?*

ANSWER. It's in Lake Erie, and the exact spot is Middle Island at 41°41' north latitude. Although many people think that the honour belongs to Pelee Island, it is only the southernmost inhabited point, lying just to the north of Middle Island.

While we're at it, here are the other extremities. The northernmost point is Cape Columbia, Ellesmere Island, at 83°7' north, which is 4,627 kilometres from Middle Island.

The eastern extremity of the country is Cape Spear, Newfoundland, at 52°37' west longitude, and 5,187 kilometres to the west is the western edge of Canada at Mount St. Elias, in the Yukon Territory, at 141° west.

Let Us
Entertain
You

Yesterday, Paul McCartney's troubles may have seemed so far away — except for that nasty rumour about his death in the 1960s. Maybe it was because so many people around the world focused on the Canadian badge he was wearing on the Beatles' Sgt. Pepper album.

Intrigued? Well, turn the pages to find out more about this Canadian link to the history of John, Paul, George and Ringo. And keep browsing to learn about the little-known Canadian who was called one of the best silent film directors of all time, the British Columbia woman who was the world's first television performer, and why we have a national newsmagazine called *Maclean's*.

QUESTION?   *What was the longest continuous running television show in Canada?*

ANSWER.   The honour goes to "Front Page Challenge," the CBC show that featured a panel of celebrities guessing the identity of people who were in the headlines. Ernie Dick, former CBC archivist who lives in Nova Scotia, claims that "Front Page Challenge" is the undisputed longest running show in the category of network programs that have kept the same format throughout their run.

Some private stations in Canada may have programs that have run longer, but he questions whether they've done so under the same name and in the same format. CFPL-TV in London, Ontario, for example, was one of the first private stations in Canada and has had a news at six o'clock program since 1953.

"Front Page Challenge" began as a summer replacement for "The Denny Vaughan Show" in 1957 and ran until the spring of 1995. Initial panelists were Gordon Sinclair, Toby Robins, Alex Barris, and Scott Young, the host was Win Barron, and the announcer was Bunny Cowan. Barron lasted less than a season and was replaced by Fred Davis.

Sinclair remained a panelist throughout his life and was later joined on the show by Pierre Berton and Betty Kennedy. Those three, and Davis, were the core of "Front Page Challenge" for many years, with a guest panelist joining them each week.

Why the longevity? "I think it was a formula that was simple," says Dick. "It could be easily adapted to whatever the stories were. I think one was always interested in what the personalities had to say and that made it interesting. I don't think the show should have been killed."

QUESTION?

Who was the Canadian described as "one of the top five movie directors of the twenties and thirties"?

ANSWER.

He appears to be almost forgotten now, but John S. Robertson was described that way in his 1964 obituary in the Escondido (California) *Times-Advocate*. Throughout his long career in silent films and later in talkies, Robertson worked with such famous actors as John Barrymore, Mary Pickford, Mary Astor, Greta Garbo, and Shirley Temple. He also turned down future stars Norma Shearer and Clara Bow when they tried to break into movies.

Robertson was born on June 14, 1878, in London, Ontario, and began his theatrical career on stage, mostly in New York. He got involved in movies as an actor in 1915, appearing in films for the Vitagraph company such as *The Combat*, *An Enemy to the King* and *His Wife's Good Name*. By 1916, Robertson was also directing.

In his heyday, Robertson was a respected and well-known director within Hollywood circles and was, as one source said, "highly acclaimed as a filmmaker for his approach of depicting sincerity without being maudlin in his delivery."

The 1920 version of *Dr. Jekyll and Mr. Hyde* is perhaps his best-known work; it's considered one of the best versions of that story ever filmed. But he also made his mark with *Tess of the Storm Country*, starring fellow Canadian Pickford.

One of the leading actors of the twenties, Richard Barthelmess, admired Robertson's work and teamed up with him in a series of films such as *The Bright Shawl*, *The Fighting Blade,* and one of the more respected movies of that era, *The Enchanted Cottage*. By 1926 Robertson was being paid $25,000 a picture, substantial money in those days for directors. He also directed films at MGM including *Annie Laurie* with Lillian Gish. Despite his fine credentials, Gish referred to the director in her autobiography as "John Robinson."

Robertson made the transition from silents into talking films directing such movies as *The Phantom of Paris*, *Little Orphan Annie*, and *Our Little Girl*, which, in 1935, was the last film of his career. During his years in the movies, Robertson directed more than forty films and acted in half a dozen.

Robertson was married to the screenwriter Josephine Lovett, who died in 1958. After his movie career, he and his wife lived for many years in Rancho Santa Fe, California, and he founded the Rancho Riding Club in 1945. Robertson is buried, along with his wife, in Mount Pleasant Cemetery, in London, Ontario, but nothing on the gravestone refers to his movie career.

The obituary did not say who the other top four directors of that era were considered to be or what criteria were used, but another Canadian, Allan Dwan, might be on that list. Dwan was born in Toronto in 1885 and directed dozens of films from 1914 to the 1960s, including *The Iron Mask*, *Sands of Iwo Jima*, *Heidi*, and *Brewster's Millions*. He died in 1981.

Mary Pickford is one of the stars who appeared in films directed by fellow Canadian John Robertson of London, Ontario.
[NAC/C16958]

QUESTION?

How did Canada's national newsweekly magazine Maclean's *get its name?*

ANSWER.

The magazine was named for John Bayne MacLean (who also spelled his name Maclean), a reporter and editor at the *Mail* in Toronto near the end of the last century. MacLean was born in 1862, and in 1887 he founded the first of his many magazines, *Canadian Grocer*. He later established other trade magazines and in doing so built the publishing empire that became Maclean-Hunter. The Hunter in the name was Horace Talmadge Hunter, who had started at the company as a printer.

MacLean bought *Busy Man's Magazine* in 1905 and in 1911 changed the name to *Maclean's*. By the 1920s, he had steered the magazine away from business and turned it into more of a Canadian nationalist publication featuring articles on a variety of subjects.

MacLean died in 1950, and about twenty-five years later the magazine went from being a monthly to the weekly we know today.

Our national news weekly was named for its founder John MacLean.
[Photo: Catherine Blake]

QUESTION?

What can you tell me about the Canadian who was the daughter of Hollywood movie director Cecil B. DeMille?

ANSWER.

Let's do a close-up of Katherine DeMille, who was in fact an orphan adopted by the famous director and played supporting roles and exotic leads in a number of films during the 1930s and 1940s.

Katherine DeMille was born in 1911 in Vancouver and was married to actor Anthony Quinn from 1937 to 1955. The couple had two children. After retiring from acting, Katherine settled in California and studied philosophy.

Movies she appeared in include: *Madam Satan*, 1930; *Viva Villa* (with fellow Canadian Fay Wray), 1934; *The Crusades*, 1935; *The Black Room*, 1935; *In Old Caliente*, 1935; *Charlie Chan at the Olympics*, 1938, *Ellery Queen, Master Detective*, 1940, *Reap the Wild Wind*, 1942 and *The Gamblers*, 1950.

QUESTION?

Is it true that Canadian actress Mary Pickford had a brother who also acted in films?

ANSWER.

Yes. Jack Pickford was born in 1896 in Toronto as Jack Smith (Mary's real name was Gladys Smith). Although he was considered too short to be a leading man, Jack acted in many silent films such as *Tom Sawyer* and *Great Expectations*. He also appeared with his sister Mary in *White Roses* and *Just Out of College*, and co-directed a couple of her films, although it seems he really didn't do much directing while on the set. They had a sister, Lottie, who also appeared in films.

Jack never achieved the fame that Mary, known to fans as America's Sweetheart, did. However, he was linked to a variety of scandals, according to a number of sources.

Scott Eyman, who wrote a biography of Mary Pickford, mentions that Jack was known to his contemporaries as a ladies' man "who was always loaded." His drinking problem is widely documented. Jack joined the Navy in 1917 and took part in a scheme that involved rich young men paying bribes to stay out of war action. For his role, Pickford came close to being dishonourably discharged.

His first marriage was to actress Olive Thomas, who scored a hit in the movie *The Flapper* in 1920. The two were described in fan magazines as "The Ideal Couple." In September of that same year, however, while in Paris on a second honeymoon with Pickford, Olive Thomas probably committed suicide. Eyman writes that while the official version was that she died of accidental poisoning, the inside story was she killed herself because Jack gave her syphilis. In fact, one of his nicknames around Hollywood was "Mr. Syphilis." Kenneth Anger writes in his book *Hollywood Babylon*, which provides a gossipy look at the movie business, that Olive Thomas had been a drug user and was in Paris trying to buy heroin for Pickford, who was an addict. Whatever the story was, her death sent shock waves through Hollywood.

Pickford continued acting, last appearing in 1928's *Gang War*, but remained a heavy drinker and dabbled in narcotics. His sister Mary spent years bailing him out of scrapes and various financial problems. He died at the age of thirty-six in Paris in January 1933 of what was described as "progressive multiple neuritis which attacked all nerve centres." More likely he died of the effects of chronic alcoholism.

QUESTION?

Where was the first play staged in Canada?

ANSWER.

The first play in this country, as well as in North America, was performed at Port Royal, Nova Scotia, on November 14, 1606. The production was called Le *Théâtre de Neptune en la Nouvelle–France* and was held to welcome home the local governor from a voyage. Actually, the play was performed on the boat that sailed out to greet his incoming ship.

QUESTION?

What can you tell me about Canadian actress Joan Miller's contribution to television?

ANSWER.

Miller, who was born in Nelson, British Columbia, in 1910 and educated in Vancouver, was the first paid professional television performer in the world, according to a history of Canadian television written by former CBC Radio and TV producer Sandy Stewart.

As a young actress, Miller won the Bessborough Trophy at the 1934 Dominion Drama Festival in Ottawa for her portrayal of the queen in the play *Elizabeth and Essex*. But she was unable to find meaningful employment in Canada and moved to the United Kingdom, where she found work as a radio actress.

Eventually, she wrote a radio sketch for herself in which she played a switchboard operator. It was performed on radio, and later Cecil Madden, the BBC's first television producer, adopted her format for the world's first television program, which was named "Picture Page."

Miller was the "Picture Page Girl" when World TV opened on November 2, 1936, and was paid £12.10 per week for the show. It was performed twice every Thursday until World War II broke out.

Miller was also the first performer to appear on a trans-Atlantic television broadcast between London and New York. One source reports that this BBC broadcast was in fact inadvertently picked up by someone in Long Island. Joan Miller went on to make a name for herself as one of the United Kingdom's most outstanding stage actresses after the war, writes Stewart, who co-created CBC's 1960s children's show "Razzle Dazzle" and was executive producer of high-school quiz program "Reach For the Top."

Miller was known to help young Canadians in Britain get roles onstage even though she never returned to Canada. Miller died in 1988.

QUESTION?

What was the Canadian connection to those "Paul McCartney is dead" rumours back in 1969?

ANSWER.

If you've got one, pull out your copy of the Beatles' *Sgt. Pepper's Lonely Hearts Club Band* album and open it up. You'll notice that in the centre spread photo McCartney is wearing an OPP (Ontario Provincial Police) badge on his left arm. The last letter is obscured, but that's what the badge signifies.

There were many supposed "clues" in evidence in 1969 hinting that McCartney had really died a couple of years before. One clue was that by playing one of the Beatles' songs backward you'd hear the message "Paul is dead." Another clue was that on the back of the Sgt. Pepper album he's the only Beatle with his back turned because the extensive facial plastic surgery for his lookalike, a man named William Campbell, wasn't finished yet. It was also said that his walking barefoot on the cover of the *Abbey Road* album was a symbol of death and that the licence plate on the Volkswagen in the background read IF-28, or what McCartney's age would have been had he lived.

The badge was another key "clue." People who believed the real Paul was dead thought the badge's letters were O.P.D., which were said to stand for "Officially Pronounced Dead." In the book *Blackbird: The Life and Times of Paul McCartney*, author Geoffrey Giuliano writes that the badge was given to McCartney as a souvenir by a Canadian cop when the Beatles were touring Canada. However, another source says a fan sent the badge to McCartney. OPP officials don't have any record of who might have provided the badge.

Eventually the rumours died down, but with sales being spurred perhaps by the event, *Abbey Road* was the Beatles' biggest selling album.

QUESTION?   *What is the best selling book ever written by a Canadian?*

ANSWER.   Hate to use an old cliché here, but ... good question. Even though we sought out a number of sources, we were unable to come up with a clear, definitive answer. The Canadian Booksellers' Association, Statistics Canada, the National Library, and the trade publication *Quill and Quire*, among others, were unable to answer the question conclusively.

In talking, however, to a number of people in the book business, including bookshop owners, we found there to be something of a consensus that it might be *Anne of Green Gables* by L. M. Montgomery. The book has been a consistent seller for about ninety years and has enjoyed popularity around the world. *Anne of Green Gables* is apparently now in the public domain, which means anyone can publish editions of it. No one, however, could supply sales figures for it.

Another suggestion put forward was *The English Patient* by Michael Ondaatje. The novel was later made into an Oscar-winning movie, which no doubt boosted sales worldwide. And one newspaper described the book *The Wealthy Barber* by David Chilton as having sold more than 1.1 million copies. It claimed the book, which provides investment advice, was the best selling title in Canada ever.

Take your pick.

QUESTION?

Why is there a Canadian magazine with the strange name Emergency Librarian?

ANSWER.

There are thousands of magazines published in North America, some with strangely funny names (how about *Shuttle Spindle* and *Dyepot* or *Chain Saw Age*?). And *Emergency Librarian* has to rank right up there. After all, what's the emergency with being a librarian (unless your book is on the verge of being overdue).

A spokesperson for the Vancouver-based magazine, however, says the name was chosen by the trade journal's founders. They were feminists who chose the name when they founded the magazine in the early seventies, because of the emergency surrounding issues to do with feminism and the lack of funding available for libraries at the time.

"We've run some notices since then to ask people if they have any suggestions for new names," the spokesperson said. "But mostly we've gotten letters saying, 'Keep the name.'"

The magazine, published bimonthly by Rockland Press, "promotes excellence in library services for children and young adults." Articles cover a wide range of topics of interest to librarians, schools and educators, including reviews of books, of videotapes and other learning materials.

QUESTION? *What is the highest-grossing Canadian movie ever?*

ANSWER.

Some people thought this movie was gross, but *Porky's* seems to be the clear winner in this category. The 1981 film, directed by Canadian Bob Clark, grossed more than (U.S.) $105 million, according to *Variety*, the American show business publication. That puts it "head and shoulders" above any other Canadian produced movie, notes a spokesperson for Astral Communications Incorporated which distributed the film. The next most successful Canadian film was probably *Meatballs*, the 1979 movie directed by Ivan Reitman and starring Bill Murray. No figures were available. *The Care Bears Movie*, released in 1985, was also popular, but *Variety* figures put it at just over $22 million. The Astral spokesperson points out, however, that this figure is based substantially on children's ticket prices, which are lower than adult prices. That means many more people went to see the movie than the figure might indicate.

Unfortunately for the Canadian film industry, box office figures for this country alone don't seem to be available. The Academy of Canadian Cinema and Television does give out a Golden Reel Award to the most successful Canadian movie at the box office each year, but the figures that determine this are vague at best.

Cineplex Odeon and Famous Players provide Canadian box office figures, but they only account for about 60 per cent of the revenues. The other 40 per cent come from independent cinemas, which aren't as forthcoming with figures, he explained.

As for *Porky's*, it was a coming-of-age film set in Florida in 1954. One critic called it a "raunchy, low-budget comedy" that has "some belly laughs." The movie spawned two sequels, neither of which were as successful.

Of course, the highest grossing movie directed by a Canadian is *Titanic*, which has earned more than $1 billion at the box office. James Cameron, the movie's director, grew up in Chippawa, Ontario.

QUESTION?

How long have the Governor General Awards for writers been around and who were the first winners?

ANSWER.

The awards, which honour Canadian writing, were introduced in 1936 by the Canadian Authors Association, which judged the awards until 1944, when an independent board was established. The first fiction winner was Bertram Brooker for his novel *Think of the Earth.*

Brooker was born in England, worked at the *Winnipeg Free Press*, and was a noted Canadian artist in the 1920s. He sold film scripts to the Vitagraph film company in the United States and wrote a couple of books on design and copy in advertising.

Think of the Earth has been described as a psychological story about a wanderer in a small Manitoba town. Brooker's last novel, *The Robber*, was written in 1949, and he died in 1955.

The non-fiction award when to T. B. Robertson for a collection of his newspaper columns from his days at the *Winnipeg Free Press*. Robertson, who was born in 1879, died in 1936, and two collections of his work were published posthumously.

The fiction and non-fiction prizes were the only two awards given out that year, but the poetry/drama category was added the following year. E. J. Pratt was the first winner of this prize for *The Fable of the Goats*.

Works in the French language weren't eligible for the awards until 1959, when André Giroux won for *Malgré tout, la joie*, a collection of short stories. Giroux had written two novels prior to that. French Canadian novelist Gabrielle Roy had won a Governor General's award back in 1947 for her well-known work *The Tin Flute*. She had won the award, however, for the English translation of her book, originally titled *Bonheur d'occasion*.

The category of juvenile literature was added in 1948, but it was later dropped. The first winner in this category was R.S. Lambert for *Franklin of the Arctic.*

Financial Facts and Pecuniary Peculiarities

Money may be the root of all evil, but it's also a pretty good source of trivia. The bottom line is that we've dug deep into our pockets of research for the dope on dollars, the expertise on earnings, and the lore on lucre.

Here are a couple of tips: It's still wise to steer clear of wooden nickels, but hang onto those blue two-dollar bills. And if you find a 1911 silver dollar in your change at the grocery store, hold on to it — you could be a millionaire.

QUESTION?   *What is Canada's most valuable coin?*

ANSWER.   Money experts tell us the coin worth the most money is the 1911 silver dollar, which is valued at more than $1 million. Its value is that high because only two were made, explains Graham Esler, curator at the Bank of Canada Currency Museum in Ottawa.

Both were patterns made by the Royal Mint in London, England, for a set which was to include the silver dollar and gold coins worth $2.50, $5.00, $10.00 and $20.00. They were authorized under the Dominion of Canada Currency Act, 1910, but for some reason the federal government of the day changed its mind and cancelled the silver dollar and the rest of the set.

A year later, however, the $5.00 and $10.00 coins were struck in gold. But nothing ever became of the 1911 silver dollar or the gold 1911 $2.50 and $20.00 coins. The 1911 silver dollar depicts King

The 1911 Silver Dollar: Canada's first million-dollar coin.

[Photo: National Currency Collection, Bank of Canada, James Zagon]

George V and is 92.5 per cent silver. It weighs 23.3 grams and is 36 millimetres in diameter.

So where are the two silver dollar patterns?

One is on display at the Bank of Canada Currency Museum, which also owns and displays the lead strike which was used to mint the pattern coins. The other, as of early 1998, was owned by American collector/dealer Jay Perrino. He purchased it for more than $1 million from Albern Coins and Foreign Exchange Limited in Calgary, which had owned it since 1996. The coin is in mint condition.

In 1997, Sean Isaacs, managing partner at Arctic Coin Ottawa Incorporated, which runs Lincoln Heights Coin & Stamp in Ottawa, predicted that the silver dollar would "become Canada's first million-dollar coin. It went to auction once with an estimated value of $500,000 and I have seen it offered for sale for $750,000."

QUESTION?   *How many millionaires are there in Canada?*

ANSWER.   At the end of 1996 (the latest date for which figures are available), 220,000 Canadians had enough assets to be considered millionaires, according to a study by Ernst & Young, a nationally known professional services firm. That's three times the number of millionaires there were in Canada in 1989, and the figure is expected to triple again by the year 2005.

The study defines millionaires as individuals with $1 million worth of investable assets. These are assets, such as stocks and bonds, mutual funds, savings accounts and term deposits, which can be easily cashed in and spent or moved to other investments. That means if you're sitting in a $1-million home or have $1 million in a company pension plan, you're not in the millionaires' club, explains Colin Deane, author of the report and a principal in Ernst & Young's International Capital Markets Group.

"A house may be worth a million but it is not spendable. It does not have a real impact on your financial situation," says Mr. Deane.

In most cases, people with a million or more in investable financial assets are older folks: Ernst & Young reports that 36 per cent were seventy years of age or older and another 24 per cent were between sixty and sixty-nine years old. Only 9.4 per cent were under forty. More than half accumulated their money through inheritances or property.

If your definition of a millionaire is someone who earns $1 million a year, then there are far fewer millionaires in Canada. The most recent Statistics Canada data shows that 2,130 people in Canada had employment income of more than $1 million in 1994. Of these wealthy Canadians, 1,190 lived in Ontario, 345 in Alberta, 320 in British Columbia, 185 in Quebec, 50 in Manitoba and 25 in Saskatchewan.

QUESTION?   *What happens to goods seized at border entry points into Canada?*

 ANSWER.   How the federal government disposes of contraband items depends on the type of goods involved, according to officials from Revenue Canada who handle customs. If you're a person who enjoys cigarettes and liquor, finding out where they end up is liable to bring tears to your eyes.

More than a billion dollars worth of trade can pass between Canada and the United States in a single day, and there are more than 100 million entries into Canada by individuals (both visitors and returning Canadians) every year, making the Canada–U.S. border one of the busiest in the world. With all of this movement of people and goods, plenty of contraband and prohibited items are discovered and seized in the course of normal operations.

In the first six months of 1997, for example, customs officials seized 4,728 cartons of cigarettes worth $68,000, 1,786 weapons worth $383,000, and were involved in 1,240 seizures of alcohol worth $181,000. But all these figures pale next to the statistics for seizures of illegal drugs such as heroin, marijuana, and cocaine. In the first half of 1997, customs made 3,776 drug seizures for a total value of $143 million.

So where does all this contraband end up?

Cigarettes are usually burned in high-heat incinerators which produce sufficient temperatures to avoid polluting the atmosphere. Where such incinerators are unavailable, tobacco products are pulverized by bulldozers at garbage dumps before being landfilled. Liquor can be disposed of in a number of ways, depending on local conditions and local services that are available, but in all cases, "it is disposed of in a way that is environmentally responsible ... often by companies that specialize in disposal of chemical waste according to the law," says Revenue Canada spokesperson Michel Cléroux. That means the booze is chemically altered and rendered environmentally harmless before being disposed of. Drugs are usually incinerated after they have been retained as evidence.

Does all of this have you wondering why the government doesn't try to get some value out of these goods — if not the illegal drugs, then at least the cigarettes and liquor, which are legal substances?

Cléroux says the main problem with selling seized liquor is the potential health risk involved. It can never be determined exactly what a bottle of contraband alcohol contains, even when it appears to be a brand-name product with the seal intact, he says, noting that smugglers are expert at producing realistic-looking products that actually contain harmful moonshine. Reports of illness or death resulting from drinking illegal liquor are not uncommon.

The situation with seized cigarettes is different. They are generally brand-name cartons that were legally produced in Canada by tobacco companies and left the country tax-free for export, before someone tried to smuggle them back into Canada. In this case, the government wants to avoid sending the wrong message. "Many Canadians would have a problem with their government becoming a tobacco merchant while at the same time running campaigns to discourage smoking," adds Cléroux.

And finally, there are the thousands of seized televisions, automobiles, diamond rings, stereos and golf clubs that are not illegal but that were seized because someone was caught trying to smuggle them and did not later pay to have the items released. These are periodically auctioned off, and yes, the proceeds go into government revenues.

There are no exact figures regarding the amount of money these auctions generate nationally, since they are conducted at a local level and the proceeds are included with other accounting items, notes Cléroux.

QUESTION?   *What can you tell me about a blue $2 bill I have in my currency collection?*

ANSWER.   Most of us probably think the only blue Canadian bill is the $5 bill. However, back in 1935, the $2 bill was blue, for a time, at least. The blue two was printed in French and English in 1935 and remained in production until 1937, when the $5 bill of the day changed colour from orange to blue.

In 1937, to avoid confusion, the Bank of Canada changed the blue $2 bill to a terra cotta colour, and it stayed that way until 1996, when it was replaced by the $2 coin, says Graham Esler, curator at the Bank of Canada Currency Museum in Ottawa.

The blue bill was the first $2 bill ever printed by the Bank of Canada and the first printed in both French and English. There were four blue $2 English bills printed for every French blue $2 bill; the notes pictured Queen Mary on the front and a transportation allegory on the back including trains, a collage of ships, an airplane and Mercury, the god of speed and commerce.

Ottawa coin and stamp dealer Sean Isaacs estimates the minimum value of an undamaged blue $2 bill at $50 for the English version and $75 for the French one. If you have one in mint condition, he says, the English one is worth $550 and the French $1,500. About 27 million blue twos were printed, but Isaacs estimates there are only several hundred still around.

QUESTION?   *Which Canadian is considered to be the founder of credit unions in North America?*

ANSWER.   Alphonse Desjardins was the man who organized the first "caisse populaire" in Quebec and then spread the word about the benefits of credit unions to other parts of Canada and the United States.

Desjardins, who was born in 1854, was trained as a journalist and published debates of the Quebec legislature in the late nineteenth century. He then became the official French-language reporter of Hansard debates in the House of Commons, a position he held from 1892 to 1917.

It was during a debate on interest rates that he came up with the idea of starting a co-operative savings and loan society that could operate on a parish level. Credit unions, as we know them today, were started in the mid-1800s in Germany. They are essentially member-owned financial institutions that provide a wide range of products and services.

Apparently, Desjardins spent several years studying, working, and even praying before at age forty-six he launched the first caisse populaire in Lévis, Quebec, in 1900. Its beginnings were humble; only a few members signed up within a month and their savings totalled just over $26. According to one source, however, one of the earlier members of this caisse populaire was Earl Grey, the governor general of Canada best known for donating the Grey Cup for football.

Desjardins had a strong social and spiritual conscience and spent a lot of his own time, money, and effort establishing credit unions that would help people from all walks of life. He took his ideas south of the border and set up the first credit union in the United States for a group of Franco-American Catholics in New Hampshire in 1909. Eventually, he set up 205 credit unions in Quebec, the rest of Canada and the United States, and by 1913 it became customary to call the new institutions "Caisses populaires Desjardins."

Edward A. Filene, a Boston merchant, was inspired by Desjardins's work and helped pass the first Credit Union Law in the United States that same year. Today there are more than 70 million credit union members in North America with assets of more than $300 billion.

QUESTION?   *How long have credit cards been in use in Canada?*

ANSWER.   Credit cards were introduced in Canada in the 1930s by oil companies which wanted us to charge our gas, oil and lube jobs. Department stores followed, and in the early 1950s, Diner's Club cards arrived from the United States.

Visa was created in 1968 as Chargex, and Mastercard came in 1973 as Mastercharge. The first bank-issued cards showed up in 1968 and are now offered by more than fifteen financial institutions such as the Royal Bank and Canada Trust.

At the end of 1997 there were 59.4 million cards in circulation in Canada, or 2.6 for every adult Canadian eighteen years or older, according to Industry Canada in Ottawa. Of those, 30.2 million were Visa or MasterCard and 29.2 million were issued by large department stores, gasoline companies and other issuers such as American Express. In total, more than six hundred companies, institutions and organizations offer cards to credit-hungry Canadians.

If all credit cards issued in Canada were laid in a line, they would stretch 5,350 kilometres, roughly the distance between Halifax and Dawson Creek, British Columbia.

The total number of credit-card transactions per year is difficult to determine, but we can tell you that in 1997 Visa and MasterCards were used nearly 897 million times, ringing up sales of $67.7 billion. Money owed on these two alone totalled $18.7 billion, compared to $17.4 billion in 1995. The value of the average MasterCard/Visa sale was $77.80 in 1995, up from the $56.79 average charged to all credit cards in 1987.

Canadians may be in love with plastic credit but not all cards leave our wallets on a regular basis. Retailers surveyed by Industry Canada indicate that about 12 million of their cards are gathering dust rather than accumulating purchases.

QUESTION? *Is income from illegal activities taxable in Canada? And are offenders who are thrown in jail required to pay tax on their ill-gotten gains?*

ANSWER. Yes and yes. Drug smugglers, car thieves, or persons who take bribes and earn, say, $250,000 from these illegal activities in a given tax year, are required to pay tax on those "earnings" — whether they're behind bars or not. Like all taxpayers, they will have the opportunity to deduct any reasonable expenses incurred to earn the income, and if they don't pay their fair share of taxes the tax department can take money from their bank accounts as payment, just as it would for non-criminal types.

And as strange as it may sound, if taxpayers are reporting income from an illegal operation, such as an escort agency that is really a front for prostitution, Revenue Canada can't rat on them to the police unless there is imminent danger to human life. "As long as these people are complying with the income tax laws, Revenue Canada will not pass judgment," affirms Revenue Canada spokesperson Michel Cléroux.

Revenue Canada often questions people on income tax matters after becoming aware via the media of events such as drug busts or court cases, says Cléroux. In the case of a taxpayer being tried for a crime, the tax department makes contact and requests that an income tax return be filed declaring all income, illegal or otherwise. If the thief doesn't file a return, Revenue Canada will do a "net worth audit" to figure out the person's income, before seeking payment.

Such was the case for a man convicted of drug trafficking between 1980 and 1988 in Saskatchewan. Although he was convicted of selling cocaine over an eight-year period, the man had never reported his income from selling the illegal drug, according to Tax Court of Canada transcripts. So, using evidence presented at his trial, Revenue Canada calculated his profit from cocaine sales to be $84,708 and billed him for the taxes, adding a hefty penalty for omitting the drug income from his personal tax returns.

For Revenue Canada, a taxpayer in jail is no different that any other taxpayer — except that he or she is easier to find.

QUESTION? *When did Canada begin using its own currency, and what kind of money did we use before dollars and coins such as nickels and dimes, came into circulation?*

ANSWER. Early currency in what was to become Canada took a variety of forms. The Bank of Canada points out that money in the form of currency and coinage began to play a part in Canadian life around 1645, in the form of a random assortment of coins from France, England, Spain and Portugal.

But some of this early money — which originated in the illicit fur-trading operations between French trappers and the merchants of New England — wasn't doing the job.

As colonization grew in the seventeenth century, it became increasingly difficult to find sufficient currency for the needs of settlers, merchants and government establishments.

This scarcity gave rise to a number of "currencies" over the years, including playing-card money, made by cutting playing cards into quarters and affixing the seal of the treasurer in wax and the autograph of the governor and the intendant, shilling notes introduced by the Canada Banking Company, army bills which had a face value of between 4 and 400 Spanish dollars, bons used by merchants to meet the need for small change, bank tokens and gold pieces.

These early forms of money were issued by the Bank of Montreal, the Bank of Quebec, the Hudson's Bay Company and provincial governments, among others.

The drive for a national currency intensified in the mid-1800s as cross-border trade with the United States increased. In 1858 the Province of Canada controlled its own currency, largely as a result of efforts by Francis Hincks, who dominated Canadian financial policy from 1848 to 1854 as inspector general and as prime minister of the province.

For years Hincks fought for the right to issue a national currency.

Following Confederation in 1867, Parliament confirmed its control of currency. Through the Bank Act of 1871, provincial currency acts were repealed wherever they were in conflict with federal control, and the Act also laid the foundations for the co-ordinated issue of currency by banks.

As banks started issuing currency under the Act, the government began the issue of 25-cent, $1 and $2 Dominion of Canada notes, with the first appearing in 1870. In 1878 the practice of countersigning $1 and $2 notes by hand began, and it continued through several issues, until as late as 1923. Dominion of Canada $4 notes appeared in 1882 and $5 notes arrived in 1912. Notes of $500 and $1,000 were introduced for general circulation in 1911. The Bank of Canada was created in 1934 and was given responsibility for issuing paper currency in Canada. The Ministry of Finance has been responsible for issuing coins since 1870.

Today, responsibility for the design and issue of banknotes rests with the Bank of Canada, subject to final approval by the minister of finance.

QUESTION?

What happens to coins that tourists throw into the pool surrounding the Centennial Flame at Parliament Hill? And where does the money collected from other public fountains, such as those found in shopping centres, end up?

ANSWER.

Brian Cooke, who is responsible for maintaining the East, West and Centre blocks and the grounds at Parliament Hill, tells us coins worth between $1,000 and $1,500 are thrown into the Centennial Flame pool every year.

The money is collected by a member of his work crew, put in buckets and sorted before being handed over to the Parliament Hill comptroller's office. Then the coins are deposited to a fund — which also contains private donations — and the money is distributed to those disabled people who help raise the profile of other disabled persons. The fund was set up by an Act of Parliament enacted on March 27, 1991, known as the Centennial Flame Research Award Act.

An application for the award must be made to the House of

Every year about $1,500 in coins is tossed into the pool surrounding the Centennial Flame at Parliament Hill.

[Photo: Randy Ray]

Commons Committee on Human Resources Development and the Status of Persons with Disabilities. To receive an award, a disabled person must write a report to the committee about the contributions of other disabled people. In 1995, the award was given to Laurie Bellefontaine of Vancouver, who wrote about Judith and Paul Thiele, a blind couple who in the late 1960s helped set up the Charles Crane Memorial Library for visually impaired people at the University of British Columbia.

Awards average about $2,500 a year, with most of the amount coming from coins tossed into the Centennial Flame pool.

As for other fountains, we'll give you two examples. At West Edmonton Mall, the largest shopping mall in the world, according to the Guinness Book of Records, about $2,000 is collected annually from the mall's fifteen fountains. After being collected by cleaning crews, the money is counted by the Parks & Attractions Cashroom and donated to the University of Alberta Bursary Fund.

At Masonville Place Shopping Mall in London, Ontario, about $1,500 in coins is collected every twelve months. A designated charity takes the money out of the fountain, rolls it up, and for its efforts receives 50 per cent of the take. The other 50 per cent is given back to the mall, which donates it to a charity of its choice.

QUESTION?   *What features in Canadian money guard against counterfeiting?*

ANSWER.   You might think paper money is redesigned solely to give it a new look. That's only part of the reason — it certainly was the case when Queen Elizabeth became reigning monarch in 1953. But the periodic redesign of bank notes is often done in order to incorporate the latest security features as a way of deterring counterfeiters, according to the Bank of Canada.

In its publication *The Story of Canada's Currency*, the bank explains that the March 1986 series of paper bills was introduced for three principal reasons: Technological advances in the printing and photocopying of coloured graphic material had made the earlier money vulnerable to counterfeiting; a bar code on notes was needed for high-speed note-sorting machines, and new features had been developed to assist the visually impaired.

Many security features in the latest designs help to identify a genuine note. On the face of the notes there are very small numerals and words barely legible to the naked eye but visible with the aid of a magnifying glass. Both sides of the notes are edged with multidirectional, fine-line patterns that appear to the naked eye as a solid block of colour. The rainbow pattern of pastel colours found on both sides of the notes is difficult to reproduce accurately, and on the back there are fine, multidirectional lines in the word Canada.

The steel engraving on bank notes continues to be an important security feature too. The dark, heavily embossed printing on the note face is characteristic of intaglio printing — a technique employed in the production of Bank of Canada notes from the beginning. It creates a certain relief, and the raised print can be felt on all but extremely worn notes.

The engraved portraits on the note faces are comprised of delicate dots and fine lines, and even a slight variation in overall contrast can result in a change in the portrait's appearance. The portraits in the latest series of notes are larger than those in earlier designs, making the portrait more of a focal point, so that variations resulting from counterfeiting will be more obvious.

The $50 bill dated 1988 and issued in 1989, as well as $20s, $100s and $1,000 bills issued between 1990 and 1993, carry a unique high-tech security feature, called an optical security device (OSD), developed by the National Research Council of Canada in Ottawa. It's an ultrathin reflective square of film on the face of the bill that changes colour from gold to green when tilted under light. This colour shift is an added indication that the bill is genuine.

The paper used in the production of bank notes is 75 per cent cotton fibres and 25 per cent wood fibres. As an additional security feature small green disks known as planchettes are embedded in the paper during manufacturing.

So how are counterfeit bills detected? All fakes exhibit defects when compared with the real thing, says the Bank of Canada. With a magnifying glass of even moderate power, it is easy to become familiar with the intricacies of note design and be able to recognize a counterfeit note by seeing, for example, print defects or the lack of planchettes.

A
Sports
Time
Out

Canada's sporting prowess has its beginnings on frozen ponds, muddy fields, and anywhere someone with a ball, a puck, or any other piece of sports paraphernalia has had a desire to play a game.

As you'll see, Canadians have become champions and innovators in all kinds of sports. You expect it in hockey and curling, but how about Canada's contributions to baseball, for example? The baseball glove, Babe Ruth's first professional home run, and the first recorded baseball game ever. That's three hits right there, and Canadians were involved in the play each time.

QUESTION?   *Can a goalie take a face-off in a hockey game?*

ANSWER.   Canadian Hockey Association rules do not specifically address the issue but another CHA manual, known as the rulebook casebook combination, states that a goaltender may not participate in a face-off, says Dave Baker of Calgary, the CHA's manager of officiating. The same is true for the National Hockey League, notes NHL spokesperson Chris Tredree.

Baker, who has been involved in hockey at the officiating level for more than twenty years, could not recall a specific incident where a goalie attempted to take a face-off. However, if the situation is addressed in the casebook it must have happened, he says. "It has been tried and tested. You can bet someone tried to read between the lines … I've seen crazier things happen."

Baker speculates that hockey coaches may have tried to use a goalie to take a draw because their netminders' extra large stick and equipment would give them an advantage when the puck was dropped. "Or maybe a goalie took the draw simply because a team was losing and the coach was being goofy," continues Mr. Baker.

The CHA casebook is used by officials to help interpret rules. "When a situation comes up it is written into the casebook and that way it saves us rewriting all of the rules," he says.

Nowhere in the NHL rule book is it clearly stated that a goalie can't take a face-off, but, according to Tredree, two rules combine to ban netminders from the face-off circles. Rule fifteen states that a hockey team consists of players and goaltenders; rule fifty-four states that face-offs are to be taken by players. In other words, forwards and defencemen can take face-offs, but goalies cannot, he says.

QUESTION?

Is it true Maurice "Rocket" Richard was not one of the hockey players chosen when the NHL named its all-time all-star players to celebrate the NHL's seventy-fifth anniversary?

ANSWER.

Fans of the Rocket were probably stunned, but Richard's name was not there among the all-star teams. The NHL chose all-time all-stars from three different eras, with the first representing the years from 1917 to 1942. On that team were Howie Morenz at center, Harvey Jackson at left wing, Charlie Conacher at right wing, Frank Brimsek in goal and King Clancy and Eddie Shore on defence.

The all-stars from the 1942 to 1967 era were Jean Beliveau at center, Gordie Howe on right wing, Ted Lindsay on left wing, Jacques Plante in goal, and Doug Harvey and Red Kelly on defence. Oddly enough, one of the all-time greats from that era, Maurice "Rocket" Richard, was not included on the list, although it can be argued that the players chosen are certainly among the greatest the game has seen.

Finally, the 1967 to 1992 team included Wayne Gretzky at center, Bobby Hull on left wing, Guy Lafleur on right wing, Ken Dryden in the net and Bobby Orr and Ray Bourque on defence. Ironically, when The Hockey News recently ranked its 50 best players of all time, Richard was number five.

QUESTION?   *When were lights first used in Canada for night football games?*

ANSWER.   The first night football game on record occurred as early as 1879, according to the Canadian Sports Hall of Fame. The game, which took place at the Montreal Lacrosse Grounds, was played under lights between the Brittania and Montreal football clubs.

Of course, the game of football was very different from today's version, and even the announcement of the game had a touch of quaintness. An ad for the game told fans there would be "Ice Cream and Strawberries Supplied on the Ground."

QUESTION?   *Who was the first Canadian woman to be a world champion in her sport?*

 ANSWER.   Canadian women burst onto the world scene in the 1928 Olympics when females were first allowed to compete in the Games. But Canada had a women's world champion a couple of years before that. Lela Brooks was a Toronto-born speed skater who won a world title in 1926 at a world championship held in Saint John, New Brunswick.

Brooks, in fact, won three world titles that year, leading the pack in the Ladies open 440-yard race, the 880-yard and the one-mile races, according to research done by the Canadian Sports Hall of Fame. Brooks wasn't yet eighteen years old when she packed her skates and set off for Saint John. Actually, the only race she didn't win at the championships that year was the 220-yard title because she fell before reaching the finish line.

Brooks had already skated her way to a number of titles prior to this championship, winning several "girls under 16" and "girls under 18" titles, starting in 1923. She won her first Canadian open and international titles in 1925 and continued her winning ways at various championships in Detroit, Pittsburgh and Quebec City over the next several years. In an eight-year span from 1923 to 1930, Brooks won more than sixty-five championships in races from 220 yards to a mile.

She held several world records, including the half-mile indoor and outdoor records, and the three-quarter mile outdoor record. In 1928 she set a world record time for skating one mile in a time of 3 minutes 13.8 seconds.

Brooks came from a family of speed skaters and began her career at the Orchard skating rink in Toronto, sometimes borrowing her mother's skates stuffed in the toe with newspaper to make them fit. Although she was only 5 foot 2 1/2 inches, Brooks was considered a fierce competitor who believed in having "the confidence you need to be a champion." Brooks skated at a time when there were no coaches, special diets or training methods to improve your skills. She usually skated by herself and would cycle with her brothers in the off-season to stay in shape.

In 1936 Brooks married Russ Campbell and moved to Owen Sound, Ontario. She decided her days of competitive skating were over and opted not to compete in the Olympic Games that year. Brooks was elected to the Sports Hall of Fame in 1970.

QUESTION?

I say Jacques Plante was the first goalie to wear a mask in the National Hockey League, but my friend disagrees. Who's right?

ANSWER.

Your friend. Although Plante is widely acknowledged as the goalie who popularized the use of a face mask in the game, he was not the first to wear one. The honour belongs to Clint Benedict of the old Montreal Maroons team. Benedict decided to wear a mask during the 1929–30 season after his nose was broken by a shot from legendary player Howie Morenz.

Benedict only wore the mask for a short time and then abandoned it. But he was the first. During his thirteen seasons, Benedict played 362 games, had a goals-against average of 2.32, and 57 shutouts. He was on four Stanley Cup winning teams, three times with Ottawa and once with the Maroons. He was elected to the Hockey Hall of Fame in 1965.

It would be about another thirty years after Benedict's career before Plante decided to don similar equipment to protect himself and change the, ahem, face of hockey.

QUESTION?   *Did Lord Grey do anything of importance other than donating the Grey Cup?*

ANSWER.   During his term as Canada's governor general from 1904 to 1911, Albert Henry George Grey was best known for donating the trophy that is the symbol of the championship of Canadian football.

Lord Grey was known to love a variety of sports, including skiing, snowshoeing and curling in the winter and golf, cricket and lawn bowling in the summer. He also enjoyed horse racing, and there was an Earl Grey Trophy for that sport as well. In addition, Grey was known as a patron of music and drama and donated many prizes in those fields during his tenure.

As for other accomplishments, Lord Grey saw his appointment as the monarch's representative in Canada as an opportunity to forge stronger links within the British Empire. He also devoted some time to improving Canada–U.S. relations and tried unsuccessfully to get Newfoundland to join Confederation. Despite all that, the Grey Cup, which cost forty-eight dollars to make, is still his main legacy. It's interesting to note that Grey wanted the Cup to "remain always under purely amateur conditions."

Lord Grey: The Grey Cup is his main claim to fame.
[NAC/C1017]

QUESTION?

Was the first baseball game played in Canada rather than in Cooperstown, New York?

ANSWER.

Good question, and one the folks in Beachville, Ontario, have been asking for some time. Some fans may not know it, but the first recorded game of baseball took place in Canada, a year before Abner Doubleday supposedly "invented" the game in Cooperstown, New York.

Beachville, about forty kilometres east of London, proudly calls itself the home of baseball in Canada because it was here on June 4, 1838, that a game of baseball, or at least a form of the game as we now know it, took place in front of several spectators.

This claim is founded on the contents of a lengthy letter published on May 5, 1886, in the Philadelphia-based *Sporting Life* magazine. The letter, entitled "A Game of Long-ago Which Closely Resembled Our Present National Game," was written by Dr. Adam Ford of Denver, Colorado, who had grown up in Beachville.

What sets Ford's letter apart from other reminiscences of early ball games is that it gives the date, describes the way the game was played, and lists the players. Most historians agree that baseball flourished before 1840 and that Doubleday's claim of having invented it is pure bunk, but there seems to be little evidence on the games' specific dates and places.

Although Ford's original letter is in the Hall of Fame in Cooperstown, New York, officials there have never formally recognized the validity of his claim for Beachville.

Two researchers from the University of Western Ontario examined the validity in a 1988 article for the *Journal of Sport History*. Nancy Bouchier and Robert Barney wrote, "The question remains: How credible is Adam Ford's letter relative to the early history of baseball? A thorough investigation of Ford himself, his sport involvement and the context of his times all suggest that his reminiscence is valuable."

Research of county records and tombstones in the Beachville area indicate most of the players would have been boys and men between the ages of fifteen and twenty-four at the time of the game, which make his recollections believable, argue the researchers.

Baseball is generally believed to be derived from the English game of rounders, and there is evidence to suggest variations of baseball were already played in the United States as early as the colonial period. Given the thousands of United Empire Loyalists who emigrated to Canada during and after the Revolution, it's likely some brought a form of baseball with them.

In fact, in her novel *Northanger Abbey*, written in the late 1790s, Jane Austen writes of a character: "and it was not very wonderful that Catherine should prefer cricket, base-ball, riding on horseback, and running about the country at the age of fourteen, to books."

But it's Ford's letter, which also includes a diagram of a five-sided playing field, that sets down for the first time the specifics of a game. As he describes it, the game had some distinguishing features: there was fair and foul ball territory, or "fair hit" and "no hit," as he called them. And the number of men on each side had to be equal before a game could be played, usually between seven and twelve players per team.

Finally, some aspects of Ford's personal life may have fueled controversy surrounding the letter. Because he was born in 1831 and

Adam Ford remembered a baseball game played in Beachville, Ontario, in 1838.

[Photo: courtesy of The Beachville District Museum]

was only a youngster when the game was played, some have questioned how a boy could have remembered such specifics. And, in addition, Ford was involved in a sensational murder scandal in St. Marys, Ontario, in 1878, when a Robert Guest, who was the secretary of the St. Marys Temperance Association, died mysteriously after drinking in Ford's office. A coroner's inquest was held behind closed doors, and Ford was not brought to trial. However, the incident prompted his move to Denver in 1880. Ford supposedly had a history of alcohol and drug problems and died virtually destitute on May 17, 1906.

In 1988, a stamp was issued recognizing 150 years of the sport in Canada. As well, a match was held that year between a team in Beachville and one from Cooperstown; it was played by the rules outlined by Ford.

QUESTION?   *Has Canada ever had the chance to show off its prowess at lacrosse at the Olympics?*

ANSWER.   We got to do it twice, winning gold medals both times, including the first one ever by athletes representing Canada (steeplechase runner George Orton won gold in 1896 but was competing for the Americans).

Lacrosse, derived from the Indian game baggataway, was an Olympic sport twice — in 1904 and in 1908. In 1904, the Winnipeg Shamrocks, an amateur team that had only been in existence for three years, represented Canada in the St. Louis Olympics. On their way to the Games, the team played exhibition matches in Minnesota and Illinois. The first one was described as "the greatest game ever played in St. Paul." There seems to be a discrepancy in the scores of the Olympic victory over a team from St. Louis. One source reported that the Shamrocks won by a score of 12 to 8 while another claimed they won a two-game series 14 to 3. Nevertheless, the Shamrocks were successful and received a raucous reception in Chicago on their way home and in Winnipeg upon their return. There was even a song about them, the first lines of which are "The Shamrock boys are corkers/They're not the kind that's slow/They're born and bred lacrossers/As we would have you know."

The 1908 team had national representation and defeated a team from Great Britain 14 to 10 to win the gold. One item of interest that shows the level of sportsmanship at the Games was that when one Canadian player broke his stick, a British player, R. G. Martin, offered to withdraw from the game until the stick could be replaced. There is another discrepancy here; this one concerns the identity of the Canadian player. One source names Frank Dixon, another says it was Angus Dillon.

Interest in the sport declined in the 1930s, and in an attempt to revive the game and also make use of arenas in the summer, it was moved indoors. This game of box lacrosse caught on with some fans in Canada and parts of the northern United States, but field lacrosse remains more popular throughout the rest of the world.

QUESTION?   *How much does the Stanley Cup weigh and what is it made of?*

 ANSWER.   Each year when you see the captain of the winning hockey team hoist the Stanley Cup over his shoulders, he is lifting about 32 pounds (14.5 kilograms for metric fans). Of course, the Stanley Cup has got larger over the years as they add bands to it to hold names. A spokesperson at the Hockey Hall of Fame says those bands only weigh one or two pounds, however, and can last a long time because "they can hold a lot of names."

The cup is silver plated and there is a kind of aluminum casting underneath.

If you think that the Stanley Cup you see being presented at the end of the finals is a replica, you're wrong. As far as the Hall of Fame and National Hockey League officials are aware, there is only one Stanley Cup and it is the real thing that is used during the presentation or at any other function.

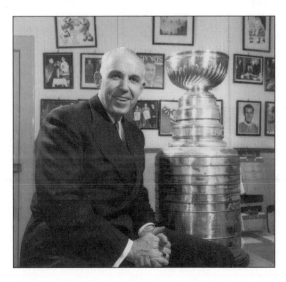

Former NHL president Clarence Campbell, with the 14.5-kilogram Stanley Cup.
[NAC/PA111399]

We've all heard of Babe Ruth, but someone told me there was a Canadian pitcher in the major leagues in the 1940s also nicknamed Babe. True?

ANSWER.

Phil Marchildon was nicknamed Babe, among other names, and had a few good seasons as a pitcher for the Philadelphia Athletics. Marchildon, born in Penetanguishene, Ontario, began his professional career in 1939 with the Toronto Maple Leafs of the International League. The next year he was called up to Philadelphia, and pitching for a dismal team, Marchildon had a record of ten wins and fourteen losses.

The next year, however, he blossomed. He had an accurate fastball and was considered one of the best pitchers in the league. He won seventeen games for one of the worst teams in baseball. The following year, though, he joined the Royal Canadian Air Force to fight in World War II; he was later shot down and spent ten months in a German prisoner-of-war camp.

He returned to baseball and despite some injuries had a remarkable year in 1946, winning nineteen games, losing nine, and helping the Athletics to fourth place. Despite his record, he lost out on the pitcher-of-the-year award to Allie Reynolds of the Yankees, who had the same won-lost record on a much better team. The following year Marchildon suffered another injury, and he pitched on and off for a few seasons but never regained his form. Marchildon, who died in 1997, is in the Canadian Sports Hall of Fame.

QUESTION?   *Who was the first American to play in the*
National Hockey League?

ANSWER.   Even though Canadians dominated the sport
for a long time, Americans and Europeans are
plentiful in today's NHL. Gerry Geran, a
forward with the Montreal Wanderers, was the
first player from south of the border to make
the NHL, according to hockey history expert
Liam McGuire of Manotick, Ontario.

Geran was born in Holyoke, Massachusetts, on August 3, 1896, and
joined the NHL in the 1917–18 season, the NHL's very first season. He
played in each of the four games the team played before its rink, the
Westmount Arena, burned down on January 2, 1918. Perhaps the fire
was a sign of the direction Geran's career would take, because he never
played in the NHL after that.

QUESTION?

What national anthems would be played if the Toronto Blue Jays met the Montreal Expos in the World Series?

ANSWER.

With the advent of interleague play in the 1997 baseball season, Canadian fans did get the chance to see the Blue Jays and Expos play in games that counted toward the standings. In the past, when the two teams met annually in exhibition games for the Pearson Cup, only "O Canada" was heard.

According to the Blue Jay organization, that tradition continued during the interleague games, when only the Canadian anthem was played. But Major League Baseball technically runs the World Series and would have final say on the choice of anthems.

There doesn't seem to be a hard-and-fast rule determining whether the "Star Spangled Banner" would also be heard, but officials from the Expos organization have said they would probably play both American and Canadian anthems at games at Olympic Stadium out of respect for the American players on the teams.

However, a spokesperson for Major League Baseball in New York says it's likely only the Canadian anthem would be heard during the World Series. That's the pattern established for interleague regular season games, and it wouldn't change for the World Series.

QUESTION?   *Which Canadian is credited with introducing the slide delivery to curling?*

ANSWER. Prior to the twentieth century, curlers would simply throw their rocks from a standing position in the hack (the area from which a stone is delivered). According to *The Joy of Curling*, the modern slide delivery got its start at the St. John's Curling Club in Winnipeg in 1930. And the book credits Ken Watson, one of the premier curlers of his time, as the father of the slide.

The story goes that one of Watson's team members forgot to put a rubber over his shoe before throwing. He ended up sliding on the ice with his stone about twenty feet. The team decided this might be a good way to throw rocks and worked hard over the next few years to perfect this style. This kind of delivery allowed for greater control, because curlers could hold onto the rocks longer and achieve a more accurate shot. The Watson team, using what became known as the "Winnipeg slide," won its first of three Canadian titles in 1936. Watson even made a film about the sport, *Magic In Curling*, which won an award at the Cannes Film Festival in 1956.

The slide was controversial from the beginning, but by the mid-1940s it had changed the style of the game. Up until the 1950s, however, there was no clear rule determining how far you could slide, and one curler, Stan Austman of Saskatchewan, once slid all the way down the ice and placed his stone on the button.

But while Watson is reported to be the creator of the slide as we know it, another source maintains he wasn't the first person to curl like this. In the book *Curling Capital*, a curler named Bob Dunbar, also of Winnipeg, was supposedly the first to effectively use the sliding delivery around the turn of the century. It's likely he wanted to slide because he liked to throw some rocks harder than others in order to take out opponents' stones. This kind of delivery gave him more momentum and helped him produce more accurate shots.

Another Winnipeg curler, Frank Cassidy, also enjoyed success with a slide in the early 1900s and into the 1920s, and he would slide a few feet farther out than Dunbar. And finally, another prominent curler, Gordon Hudson, who was from Kenora, Ontario, became a dominant player in the 1920s, sliding several feet farther than Cassidy did before releasing his rock. In fact, Watson used to watch Hudson curl as a way of learning the game.

The slide delivery in curling was developed by several Canadians over the years.

[Photo: Catherine Blake]

QUESTION?   *When was the penalty shot introduced to professional hockey?*

 ANSWER.   Hockey history expert Liam McGuire tells us that hockey's most exciting play was introduced in the Pacific Coast Hockey League in the 1916–17 season by league founders Lester and Frank Patrick. The first documented use of the shot was in a playoff game in 1922, when Babe Dye of Toronto St. Pats broke in on netminder Harry Holmes of the Vancouver Millionaires but failed to score.

In those days there were two types of penalty shots — major shots and minor shots, says McGuire. A major was called when a player was clearly hauled down while having a clear shot at scoring. During the penalty shot, the player could skate right in on the goalie, as is the case today. A minor penalty shot was called when the puck was dislodged from a player's stick but the player wasn't pulled down. In this case, the player taking the shot had to shoot before reaching a line on the ice twenty-six feet from the net.

The National Hockey League introduced the penalty shot in 1934–35. The first one was taken by Armand Mondou of the Montreal Canadiens who was stopped by Toronto Maple Leafs' goaltender George Hainsworth. The first successful penalty shot took place just three days later on November 13, 1934, when St. Louis Eagles player Ralph (Scotty) Bowman, no relation to the great NHL coach, beat Montreal Maroons goalie Alex Connell.

Just in case you're wondering, goalies win penalty shot battles more often than shooters, in the National Hockey League, at least. Since 1938, statistics show that in 61.8 per cent of penalty shots, the netminder makes the save. Prior to expansion in 1967–68, only 115 penalty shots were awarded, but since then 455 penalty shots have been attempted.

QUESTION?   *Who was the Canadian who invented the baseball glove?*

ANSWER.   Some baseball historians suggest Art "Foxy" Irwin invented the baseball glove, while others more cautiously describe him as having "popularized" the glove. Another source credits Irwin with inventing the "infielder's glove."

At any rate, Irwin, also known as "Doc," was a baseball pioneer from Canada. He was born in Toronto on February 14, 1858, and raised in Boston. He took up baseball and by 1880 was one of the best shortstops in the game. At this point in the game's development, infielders like Irwin caught balls with their bare hands.

Around 1883, however, a hard-hit ball broke two fingers on Irwin's left hand, and rather than waiting for them to heal, he bought a buckskin glove that was a bit too big, added some padding, inserted his fingers and kept playing. Within a couple of years several players were using what was known as the "Irwin Glove." For what it's worth, Irwin had an outstanding fielding percentage, well over .800 consistently. But Chip Martin, a London, Ontario, reporter and author who has been researching the early days of baseball, says a catcher, named Phil Powers, with the London Tecumsehs started using a primitive glove in 1878. Others were also beginning to try out new equipment at the time.

Nevertheless, Irwin was an interesting figure. He batted left, threw right, was 5 foot 8 1/2 inches and weighed 158 pounds. He played with a variety of teams in his thirteen-year career. In addition to playing a role in the introduction of the baseball glove, he led a players' revolt in 1890, managed a team in Toronto in the 1890s, was a National League umpire in 1902, introduced professional baseball to Cuba, and initiated the system of baseball scouting.

Irwin was apparently depressed as a result of having to handle two marriages at the same time, and on July 16, 1921, he jumped overboard into the Atlantic Ocean and drowned while sailing on the liner *The Calvin Austin* between New York and Boston.

QUESTION?

Has a hockey player ever been charged with murder after injuring another player during a hockey game?

ANSWER.

Charles Masson of the Ottawa Vics of the Federal Amateur Hockey League was slapped with a murder charge after Cornwall player Owen McCourt died in hospital in March 1907, less than a day after being hit over the head by a stick during a melee.

The charge was later reduced to manslaughter, but at Masson's trial in April several witnesses claimed another player's stick had struck McCourt just prior to Masson's involvement in the fight, writes Brian McFarlane in his book *50 Years of Hockey 1917 – 1967: An Intimate History of the National Hockey League.* Masson was later acquitted. Interestingly enough, Masson only played two games in his life, one in 1906 and this one in 1907. There's no record of his scoring any goals or assists.

Another high-profile death directly related to a hockey game was that of Bill Masterton who played with the Minnesota North Stars of the National Hockey League. Masterton died in hospital on January 15, 1968, after hitting his head on the ice three days earlier during a game against the Oakland Seals. The fall occurred after Masterton was sandwiched by Seals' players Larry Cahan and Ron Harris.

Masterton played thirty-eight games before he was hit in that game against the Seals. His career totals were four goals and eight assists for twelve points. In his honour, the Bill Masterton Memorial Trophy is given out annually to the NHL player who best exemplifies the qualities of perseverance, sportsmanship and dedication to hockey.

QUESTION?   *Did Babe Ruth's home-run prowess get its start in Canada?*

ANSWER.   Yes. As a minor-league pitcher with the Providence Grays, Ruth hit his first professional home run (and only one while he was in the minor leagues) in Toronto. The three-run homer over the right-field fence at the Island Stadium near Hanlan's Point came in the sixth inning of a game against the Toronto Maple Leafs on September 5, 1914.

In the course of the game Ruth pitched a one-hit shutout, with the Grays winning 9 to 0. He later went on to pitch in the major leagues with the Boston Red Sox and then became renowned as a slugger with the New York Yankees. Ruth returned to Toronto in 1923 with the Yankees for an exhibition game against the Leafs and hit another home-run ball that apparently ended up in Lake Ontario.

A newspaper account of the time described that homer as soaring "until it looked as if it would never come down, but it finally stopped sailing and fell out of sight back of the bleacher wall into the bay with a mighty splash."

There are other Canadian connections to Ruth's baseball career. When he was growing up in Baltimore, Ruth learned baseball from a Brother Matthias, a Canadian who grew up as Martin Boulier in Lingan, Cape Breton. He was a teacher at St. Mary's Industrial School for Boys in Baltimore, where Babe met him. Matthias was a big man who could hit balls out of the park with one hand on the bat. "He was the greatest man I've ever known," Ruth would say. "I think I was born as a hitter the first day I ever saw him hit a baseball."

When Ruth started as a pitcher with Boston in 1914, he gave up his first hit to Jack Graney, a native of St. Thomas, Ontario, then playing for Cleveland. Ruth told some folks his wife, Helen Woodford, was Canadian, but she was actually from Boston. Joe Lannin, the Boston Red Sox owner who signed Ruth to his first major-league contract, was also Canadian.

QUESTION?   *Who was the first player ever to be drafted into the National Hockey League?*

ANSWER.   The NHL conducted its first draft in 1963 and the first player picked was Garry Monahan, who was drafted by the Montreal Canadiens. The draft included all amateur players seventeen years of age and older who were not on teams sponsored by the six teams that made up the league at the time, explains Rick Davis, an archivist at the Hockey Hall of Fame in Toronto.

Monahan was drafted from the Toronto-based St. Michael's College hockey organization, which has spawned many hockey greats, including Joe Primeau, Dave Keon, Red Kelly, Frank Mahovlich and Eric Lindros. He played junior hockey with the Peterborough Petes before jumping to the NHL, where he skated with Montreal, Detroit Red Wings, Los Angeles Kings, Vancouver Canucks and Toronto Maple Leafs.

The second player taken in the 1963 draft was Peter Mahovlich, who later joined the Red Wings. Coincidentally, about three years into their careers, the two swapped teams, with Monahan going to Detroit and Mahovlich to Montreal. Monahan retired from the NHL after the 1978–79 season. During his twelve-year career, Monahan played 748 regular season games, scored 116 goals and 169 assists for 285 points and had 484 penalty minutes. When we tracked Monahan down, he was selling real estate in West Vancouver.

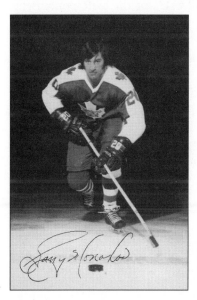

Garry Monahan, the first player ever drafted to play in the National Hockey League.
[Photo: The Collection of Garry Monahan]

Canadians such as Larry Walker and Ferguson Jenkins have left their mark in modern-day baseball, but how did our homegrown players fare in the early days of the sport?

Without taking any credit away from Walker, Jenkins and other great Canadian ballplayers, we can tell you many Canucks have blazed paths of glory in major-league baseball. At times, in fact, several have outperformed the game's biggest names, says Jim Shearon of Kanata, Ontario, whose book *Canada's Baseball Legends* chronicles the Canadian contribution to the game from 1879 to the present.

To this day, Tip O'Neill, an outfielder from Woodstock, Ontario, still boasts the highest batting average in baseball history — .492 for St. Louis in 1887. Born in Brantford, Ontario, O'Neill started his career as a pitcher for the New York Metropolitans in 1883. Like Babe Ruth later, O'Neill switched to the outfield and played for nine seasons. In 1887, when walks were counted as hits, he batted .492. Even after the walks were deducted, he hit .435. The latter average was bettered in 1894, when Hugh Duffy hit .438, but O'Neill's .492 at the plate remains the best-ever batting average.

Then there was George "Mooney" Gibson, a native of London, Ontario, who set a major-league record by catching 133 consecutive games for the Pittsburgh Pirates in 1909. Known as a light hitter, Gibson crowned his season by outhitting Ty Cobb .240 to .231 in the World Series to help Pittsburgh upset Detroit. He later managed in the big leagues.

When, in 1910, the spitball was legal, Russell Ford found that a scuffed baseball curved erratically, according to Shearing. He made the discovery after an errant pitch struck a wooden pillar. While opponents thought he was spitting on the ball, Ford, a native of Brandon, Manitoba, used emery paper to scuff baseballs and won twenty-six games as a rookie pitcher for the New York Yankees.

St. Thomas, Ontario, native Jack Graney started his career as a pitcher with the Cleveland Indians but was injured by a line drive at

New York and became an outfielder. He was the first batter to face Babe Ruth, when Ruth made his pitching debut with the Boston Red Sox in 1914. On June 26, 1916, he became the first baseball player to wear a number on his uniform, and he was the first former player to broadcast a major-league baseball game after fourteen years with the Indians.

In 1941, Ted Williams batted .406 and Joe DiMaggio hit safely in 56 consecutive games but Jeff Heath, an outfielder from Fort William, Ontario, had more hits than either of them. Heath, who was chosen to play the outfield in the 1941 all-star game alongside Williams and DiMaggio, ended the season with 199 hits, while DiMaggio had 193 and Williams 185.

The first black player to appear on a baseball card was born in Canada. He was Jimmy Claxton, who was born in British Columbia in 1892, but moved as a child to Tacoma, Washington. Eventually, he played in the Pacific Coast League with the Oakland Oaks. In 1916 he appeared on the Zee-Nut series of baseball cards, thus becoming the first black player to appear on a card.

People Make Canada Tick — Crazy Canucks? Not Really!

If we asked you what Harry Houdini, Blackbeard the pirate, the Hardy Boys, *The King and I*, and the robber who coined the phrase "Hands Up" have in common, would you say Canada?

You should, because all these people or characters have interesting connections to our country. If *People* magazine had been around for a hundred years or so, it would have had to send a team of correspondents to Canada to dig up this kind of juicy information. Don't worry, we've done that and more.

QUESTION?   *Who was Canada's first female medical doctor?*

ANSWER.   The woman generally considered to have the right to this title is Emily Howard Stowe. Inspired by her husband's illness from tuberculosis, Stowe studied medicine at the New York Medical College for Women. The lifelong champion of women's rights and former Brantford, Ontario, teacher was forced to study south of the border, because no Canadian medical college would accept a female student.

Stowe, also credited with being the first woman principal in Canada, graduated in 1867 and set up a doctor's office in Toronto, becoming the first woman to practise medicine in Canada. She attracted many women patients, but a law was passed in Ontario requiring all doctors trained in the United States to attend lectures at a medical school here.

Stowe, therefore, was practising without a licence, which was allowed at the time. But Stowe wasn't the first to get her licence once that regulation was introduced. Dr. Lawrence Segal of Toronto, who has researched this topic, notes that Jennie Kidd Trout was the first licenced woman physician. She earned that title in 1875, while Stowe didn't get her licence until 1880. And there was another woman who was licenced to practise midwifery, and she might have been considered a doctor at the time as well, he points out.

"Of course, if you're going to say who was the first doctor, it was probably some Native North American," says Segal. "But if you qualify it as who was the first Canadian woman licenced as a doctor, then it's Trout."

Not that Stowe doesn't have her own claims to fame. In her book *The Indomitable Lady Doctors*, author Carlotta Hacker indicates that Stowe's struggle to enter the profession led her to help set up the Women's Medical College in Toronto in 1883. She also founded the Toronto Women's Literary Club, Canada's first suffrage group, and was principal founder and first president of the Dominion Women's Enfranchisement Association in 1889.

QUESTION?

What is the link between shipping entrepreneur Samuel Cunard and the infamous pirate "Blackbeard"?

ANSWER.

Cunard, a native of Halifax, was an entrepreneur and shipping magnate, who in the early 1800s ruled the North Atlantic with a shipping line that had been established by his father, Abraham. The shipping, whaling, lumber, coal and iron businesses later made Cunard a very wealthy man.

However, legend has it that the root of the family fortunes was a pirate's money. Here's the story: In 1718, Thones Kunders, Samuel's great-great-grandfather (his name was changed to Cunard when a careless surveyor misspelt it on a land deed) is said to have been smoking his pipe late one night when he saw a handful of pirates burying a treasure chest near his home in Pennsylvania. According to the conversation he overheard, the treasure hoard had been taken from legendary scoundrel Edward "Blackbeard" Teach, an English sailor turned pirate.

Samuel Cunard was connected to an infamous pirate, Blackbeard.
[NAC/PA124022]

About a year later, Cunard returned to the scene and with some brief spadework uncovered a small brass-studded chest, which, when unearthed, proved to be brimming with gold coins. He used the money to buy a coastal vessel, which was to become the first of what later became a large and successful merchant fleet.

Subsequently, Abraham Cunard continued his father's shipping tradition in Halifax and eventually handed the company to his son Samuel, who in the early 1800s turned the shipping company into the unchallenged leader in the North Atlantic. Samuel's shipping activities involved mainly sailing ships, but he also had experience in early steam navigation as a shareholder in the wooden paddle wheeler the *Royal William*, which in 1833 made a historic crossing of the Atlantic largely under steam power.

Later, as the Cunard Steamship Company Limited, the firm absorbed competitors, including the White Star Line, and was the owner of liners such as the *Lusitania* and the *Queen Elizabeth II*. Samuel Cunard died in London, England, in April 1865, with a fortune estimated by some at £350,000 but by others at considerably more.

In his biography of Samuel Cunard, author John M. Bassett writes: "The story of Cunard and Teach's gold can, of course, not be proven. If it is true, it is easy to see why Cunard would not want it to become common knowledge. If just a family legend, it is at least a pleasantly ironical one — that a great shipping line was founded with a pirate's money."

QUESTION?   *Who was the man who called himself the Poet Laureate of Canada?*

ANSWER.   We'd like to tell you that he was one of our greatest poets, but, unfortunately, the man who labelled himself this way is referred to as one of the worst verse writers this country has produced.

James Gay was born in 1810 and died in 1891. During his writing career he penned odes to Queen Victoria and Canada's governors general. Gay lived in Guelph, Ontario, and was renowned for owning a two-headed horse. And while he sought fame and fortune through his poetry, he at least had the sense to know what people wanted the most. Gay charged five cents for his poems, but ten cents to anyone wanting a view of his horse.

Gay was also known to speak in rhyme whenever he had the chance, greeting people with such lines as "Nice day, nice day, so says Canada's poet, James Gay."

QUESTION?   *Is there a Canadian connection to the holdup command "Hands Up"?*

ANSWER.   The bandit believed to be first to order innocent victims to raise their hands over their heads before stealing their money and valuables was Bill Miner. Although he was an American, Miner certainly left his mark in Canada, at one point being the subject of a heated debate in the House of Commons.

But more on that later.

To determine who first uttered the command "Hands Up," we turned to the writings of three reputed Old West crime authors. Their answers were less than definitive, but the lore surrounding the exploits of Miner has all sorts of Canadian connections.

In *Tales of the Golden Ears Illustrated*, by Donald Ender Waite, the author reports: "The soft-spoken command 'hands up,' followed by several apologetic remarks during the actual holdup, became a Miner trademark and earned him the nickname 'Gentleman Bandit.'" But in the much more detailed book *The Grey Fox*, authors Mark Dugan and John Boessenecker write: "Legend has it that Miner was the first to use the term 'hands up!' but detailed accounts of his first robberies provide no evidence to support this assertion."

So, the jury is still out. But the verdict is certainly in on Miner's contribution to early crime in Canada. And he's as guilty as can be.

Miner, who was born on the outskirts of the town of Onondaga, Michigan, on December 27, 1846, is known as one of the great bandits of his time and, to this day, remains a legend in the Pacific Northwest. In the eyes of some, Miner, who came to be known as "the last of the old-time bandits," was close in popularity to Robin Hood, Jesse James and Billy the Kid.

His wasn't an entirely successful career, however: From age eighteen, when he pulled his first job — the theft of twenty-one horses and a mule on July 31, 1863, from a prosperous Los Angeles County ranchero — he spent thirty-seven years in prison, with some of his jail time

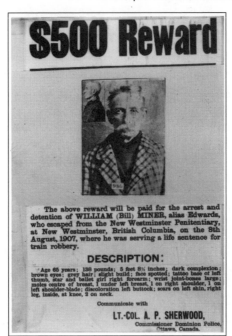

$500 Reward

The above reward will be paid for the arrest and detention of WILLIAM (Bill) MINER, alias Edwards, who escaped from the New Westminster Penitentiary, at New Westminster, British Columbia, on the 8th August, 1907, where he was serving a life sentence for train robbery.

DESCRIPTION:

Age 65 years; 138 pounds; 5 feet 8½ inches; dark complexion; brown eyes; grey hair; slight build; face spotted; tattoo base of left thumb, star and ballet girl right forearm; wrist joint-bones large; moles centre of breast, 1 under left breast, 1 on right shoulder, 1 on left shoulder-blade; discoloration left buttock; scars on left shin, right leg, inside, at knee, 2 on neck.

Communicate with

LT.-COL. A. P. SHERWOOD,
Commissioner Dominion Police,
Ottawa, Canada.

Train robber Bill Miner's mug on a wanted poster, circa 1907.

[Photo: Vancouver Public Library, photograph number 1786]

behind bars in Canada. "As Miner's time in prison attests," write Dugan and Boessenecker, "he was good at being caught."

In a career of crime that spanned more than forty-five years, Miner made a name for himself as a robber of stage coaches and trains, but he also stole clothing, as well as watches, and robbed houses. He never killed anyone and was a folk hero, cheered on occasionally by the public because he only robbed corporations.

It was a robbery involving a venerable Canadian corporation that helped Miner enter Canadian folklore. On September 10, 1904, he and two accomplices robbed a Canadian Pacific Railway train at Mission Junction, British Columbia, forty miles east of Vancouver. Their take was $7,000 in money and gold and $300,000 in bonds and securities (worth more than $5 million in today's dollars.) It was Miner's first successful train holdup and Canada's first train robbery. And during the robbery, according to Dugan and Boessenecker, Miner used the command "Hands Up!"

Within days, the CPR and the B.C. government had offered rewards totalling $11,500 for the arrest of the bandits. On May 9, 1906, Miner and two helpers robbed a Canadian Pacific train at Ducks, British Columbia, 16 miles east of Kamloops, leaving the scene with only $15.50. Less than a week later, on May 14, 1906, Miner and his fellow desperadoes were captured near Douglas Lake, B.C. On June 1, 1906, all three were tried and convicted in a courtroom at Kamloops, B.C., and Miner was sentenced to life imprisonment. He was fifty-seven years old at the time.

As was often the case in his storied career, Miner wasn't in jail for long. On August 8, 1907, according to *The Grey Fox*, Miner, partly crippled and sixty-one years of age, was allowed to escape from the Canadian prison as part of a deal prison authorities and the CPR had concluded in order to recoup the $300,000 in securities. The escape raised the hackles of Parliamentarians in the House of Commons when Wilfrid Laurier was prime minister, with allegations of cover-ups and collusion flying every which way.

In a speech in the Commons, Laurier said: "It was a shock when we heard, and we heard it with a good deal of shame also, that he [Miner] had subsequently been allowed to escape from the penitentiary." Shortly thereafter, however, the government refused to institute a full inquiry into Miner's escape, arguing that vague rumours were not grounds for an investigation.

Bill Miner was never caught in Canada and the missing securities were never recovered, according to Dugan and Boessenecker.

In the spring of 1910, Miner and two accomplices robbed a train in Georgia and made off with about $2,200. Four days later all were caught, and on March 3, 1911, at age sixty-four, Miner was sentenced to twenty years in a Georgia prison. After two more escapes, Miner died on September 2, 1913, at age sixty-six at Milledgeville prison farm in Georgia, never having killed anyone or firing a shot from a gun.

As a show of support for the man with the dim view of big business, the citizens of Milledgeville paid all his funeral expenses. The local citizenry had never before bestowed such treatment on a prisoner.

The story of Bill Miner was later made into a movie, *The Grey Fox*, by Mercury Pictures Incorporated of Vancouver, starring Richard Farnsworth as Miner. It was also chronicled in a song written by Canadian singer Ian Tyson.

QUESTION?   *Is there any record of the first non-Native child born in what is now Canada?*

ANSWER. As Farley Mowat speculates in his writings on the Vikings, the first such child born here would probably have been a boy named Snorri. The child was born around the year 1003 or 1004. The parents were Thorfinn Karlsnefi, a Viking seaman and trader, and his wife Gudrid, who accompanied him on an expedition to what is now Labrador and Newfoundland when she was six months pregnant. The colonists spent a long cold winter in this area, and it was then that the child was born.

According to Mowat, the child was probably named for Snorri Thorbrandsson, who was Thorfinn's closest friend. Eventually Thorfinn and Gudrid went to Greenland, where they spent time with Erik the Red, and then returned to Iceland.

QUESTION? *Did Evita, the wife of Argentine dictator Juan Peron, secretly visit Canada shortly before her death to receive treatment for cancer?*

ANSWER. The rumour of Eva Peron, commonly known as Evita, being smuggled into Canada for cancer treatment has been part of the London, Ontario, medical establishment rumour mill for more than forty-five years.

The story goes that Dr. Ivan Smith, head of the Ontario Cancer Foundation's London Clinic at the time, treated Evita with Cobalt 60 therapy, which he had introduced in late October of 1951. Whether he did or not, Eva Peron died on July 26, 1952.

Few people believe the rumour is true, and there doesn't seem to be any solid evidence to back it up, but it persists to this day. That Evita's life has been made into a popular Broadway musical and a Hollywood movie starring Madonna, might also explain the continuing fascination with Eva Peron.

London, Ontario, and Dr. Smith made headlines in late 1951 because London was one of the first places in the world to have the new cobalt cancer treatment technology. "New Cancer Weapon Hailed," said a headline on October 27, 1951. A story in the *London Free Press* that same day mentioned Eva Peron's battle with "her illness."

When we contacted the London Regional Cancer Clinic's records department, a spokesperson there commented that the rumour is still circulating and that people occasionally investigate it. Several doctors who have come on staff have looked into the Evita rumour, but so far the clinic has found no evidence in its records that she was in London for the treatment. There is the possibility she came under a different name or that the records have been removed, but no one can confirm that.

Cameron Johnston, a London freelance journalist, has researched the story thoroughly. According to him, a couple of doctors who knew Smith, who died in 1962, always had a "mischievous glint" in their eyes when talking about the rumour. "It probably started as a lark and they just kept running with it."

It's also possible Smith himself started the rumour because the treatment was expensive and any financial support he could get would have been beneficial, Johnston added. A London historian, who has also since died, claimed he was in Smith's office when a call came from Evita's doctors seeking help.

Dr. John Orchard, a retired physician, who also knew Smith, doesn't believe the story even though London did have this technology. "The cancer clinic in London keeps the most meticulous records, but I suppose if she came, which I personally don't believe she did, they probably would have wiped them out, don't you think?... It is an interesting story."

QUESTION?   *What can you tell me about Louis Cyr, a Canadian strongman from Quebec?*

ANSWER.   Cyr, a native of St. Cyprien de Napierville, southeast of Montreal, weighed 18 pounds at birth, and by the age of nine he was carrying 100-pound calves under his arm. At age eleven, he weighed 140 pounds.

At some unknown point he became a "professional strongman" and began travelling in carnivals, challenging all comers to contests of strength. In one such event, he outmatched another muscleman by lifting a 480-pound stone.

After working as a Montreal policeman, Cyr embarked on tours of Europe and the United States, where he challenged other strongmen to weight-lifting contests, always winning. Ottawa historian Hugh Halliday says Cyr's feats included: lifting 551 pounds with one finger; hoisting a platform on his back that weighed 4,100 pounds and his greatest lift, raising 4,337 pounds of weights on his back in 1895 in Boston.

Halliday reports that Cyr used to eat six pounds of meat at dinner and that his zest for food and drink ultimately killed him. Around the

year 1900, he developed Bright's disease, a body-wasting malady that would take his life. A number of plaques and monuments in Quebec commemorate various stages of Cyr's career, notes Halliday.

Strongman Louis Cyr once lifted 551 pounds with one finger.

[NAC/C86343]

QUESTION?   *Did a Canadian kill famed escape artist*
Harry Houdini?

ANSWER.   Through the years, the story has been told that when Houdini visited Montreal in October 1926 he was hit in the stomach by a McGill University student. Houdini died in Detroit, Michigan, less than two weeks later, and many have said it was the blow he took that ultimately caused his death.

But who was this student, why did he hit Houdini, and was he ultimately responsible for the great magician's death?

Houdini was visiting Montreal to perform at the Princess Theatre and was invited to McGill by the dean of the Faculty of Psychology to talk to students. There are varying descriptions of just when and how Houdini came into contact with the student who hit him, and, in fact, some news reports of the day stated that Houdini was hit in a friendly sparring match with a newspaper reporter.

The student whose name appears most often in published reports, however, was Jocelyn Gordon Whitehead of British Columbia who was either an arts student or studying theology at McGill. According to the book *The Life and Many Deaths of Harry Houdini* by Ruth Bradon, a number of students asked if it was true that Houdini could withstand a blow to the stomach without feeling any pain. Houdini said yes. One eye witness, Jack Price, said Whitehead hit the escape artist about four times before Houdini asked him to stop. Price said it appeared Houdini was in pain because he'd had no opportunity to prepare his muscles for such blows. Whitehead was apparently more than six feet tall, quite strong and probably did catch Houdini off guard.

Houdini left Montreal shortly thereafter and went by train to Detroit. By the time he arrived there, he was feeling ill and saw a doctor. He was diagnosed with acute appendicitis but still managed to perform in a show. He was rushed to hospital the next morning and had his appendix removed by a Dr. Charles Kennedy. Houdini remained in hospital for a few more days, apparently getting better at one point and then taking a turn for the worse. He died on October 31 of what doctors described as peritonitis brought on by a ruptured appendix. Adding another Canadian connection to all this, Dr. Kennedy concluded that Houdini's appendix must have ruptured sometime on the train ride near St. Thomas, Ontario.

Although people then assumed Whitehead's blows had caused the death, Bradon explains the consensus today is that this would have been medically impossible. She says such a blow might have ruptured the large intestine but not the appendix. She believes Houdini was already suffering from appendicitis before he reached Montreal.

As for Whitehead, information provided by McGill University's archives suggests the student was never investigated for any wrongdoing in Houdini's death. Also, a professor of psychology denied that any punching took place after Houdini delivered his lecture at McGill. It's possible, however, that the blow took place at a different time, in Houdini's dressing room. In the end, Houdini's widow appears to have been the beneficiary of an insurance policy worth twenty-five thousand dollars that doubled if the escape artist's death was deemed accidental rather than from an aggressive action. Her New York lawyers inquired about the Montreal incident, but signed an oath declaring that Whitehead had no intention of hurting Houdini. Apparently, Whitehead later accepted a job as a religious minister in the United States and disappeared into anonymity.

QUESTION?   *What was author Charles Dickens doing in Canada in the 1840s?*

ANSWER.   Dickens was already a celebrated author by then, having written such classics as *Oliver Twist* and *A Christmas Carol*. And while many of his most popular books still lay ahead, Dickens began in the early 1840s to toy with the notion of visiting North America for a book tour. He had even received a letter from American writer Washington Irving saying that such a visit would be "a triumph… as was never known in any Nation."

Early in 1842 he boarded the steamship *Britannica* and set off for his visit. Although he was primarily going to the United States, the ship first stopped in Halifax, where Dickens was given a warm reception. He visited several American cities such as Boston, New York and Philadelphia, giving readings and making observations of his travels. He was becoming acutely aware by then of his Englishness, how he differed from Americans, notes his biographer Peter Ackroyd. By late spring Dickens had made his way to Niagara Falls, and according to Ackroyd, "he was free at last. He had left America behind." From there he and his wife, Catherine, visited Toronto for a few days, which he described as a town "full of life and motion, bustle, business and improvement. The streets are well paved, and lighted with gas; the houses are large and good; the shops excellent." He then travelled to Montreal, where a British garrison was stationed, and participated in some theatricals by the Garrison Amateurs there. He returned to the United States and set sail for England in June.

One of Dickens's sons, Francis Jeffrey, came to Canada in 1874 to join the Northwest Mounted Police and had what has been described as an "unspectacular career" until 1886. He died that year in Moline, Illinois, after being invited there to lecture.

QUESTION?   *What is the Canadian connection to the popular Hardy Boys series?*

ANSWER.   If this has been a mystery to you, consider it solved. Although Leslie McFarlane didn't create The Hardy Boys, he is responsible for writing the first twenty or so books in the series under the pen name Franklin W. Dixon. Not only did McFarlane write them, he wrote them while living in Canada, notably in Haileybury, Ontario, where he had grown up, and later in Montreal.

In the spring of 1926, McFarlane, who had worked for newspapers in Canada and the United States (and who is the father of hockey broadcaster and author Brian McFarlane), saw an ad for an "Experienced Fiction Writer" being sought by the Stratemeyer Syndicate of New Jersey. The syndicate, owned by Edward Stratemeyer, was responsible for a series of fictional heroes such as Dave Fearless. McFarlane wrote a couple of Dave Fearless books, under the pseudonym Roy Rockwood, but didn't enjoy them much. The syndicate would send him the outline as well as the plot of the book and he had to fill in the rest. For that he received $100 and no royalties.

The Franklin W. Dixon of Hardy Boys fame was really Canadian Leslie McFarlane. [Photo: Catherine Blake]

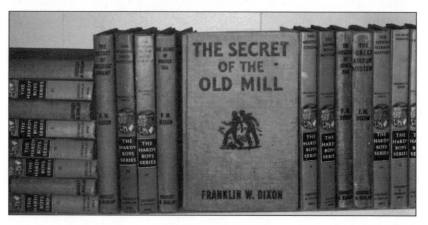

Stratemeyer then asked him to begin work on a new series he'd conceived called The Hardy Boys. McFarlane's pay was hiked to $125 (it went up slightly in later years, but again he received no royalties) and he would be writing from outlines and plots provided by the syndicate. Franklin W. Dixon was born, and McFarlane started with *The Tower Treasure*.

The books, which feature brothers Joe and Frank Hardy, sons of the famous detective Fenton Hardy, are set in the fictional town of Bayport. By the time McFarlane began writing them, he had returned to northern Ontario. He had moved back to Haileybury by the time he started on the third book in the series, *The Secret of the Old Mill*.

In his autobiography, *The Ghost of the Hardy Boys*, McFarlane says he looked upon the books as a job and didn't pay much attention to them once they were released. He faithfully followed the outlines, but the nuances he added to the characters are probably one reason why the books were so popular.

McFarlane also wrote a couple of volumes of The Dana Girls, under the pen name of Carolyn Keene ("author" of the Nancy Drew mysteries). He continued writing Hardy Boys books through the thirties and forties, completing his last one, *The Phantom Freighter*, while in Nova Scotia directing a film.

McFarlane didn't just write Hardy Boy books; he also made a name for himself penning short stories, radio plays, novels, and film scripts. A documentary for which he wrote the script, *Herring Hunt*, was nominated for an Academy Award.

He claimed it wasn't until the 1940s that he found out the Hardy Boys were apparently the best-selling boys books in the world. The books have been ghostwritten by others since then, and McFarlane's original stories have been rewritten and updated. He died in 1977.

QUESTION?   *Who was the first Canadian to fly an*
airplane?

ANSWER.   Many believe John McCurdy of Baddeck,
Nova Scotia, was the first Canadian to leave
the ground in an airplane but that's not the
case. Frederick Walker "Casey" Baldwin was
Canada's first flyer.

Baldwin, a distinguished engineer and a
graduate of the University of Toronto, worked
on the problems of human flight with McCurdy and telephone inventor
Alexander Graham Bell, whose summer home was in Baddeck.

The first biplane built by Bell, McCurdy, Baldwin and two Americans
was tested at Hammondsport, New York, on March 12, 1908. Baldwin
took the controls of the Red Wing before dozens of spectators, piloted
the craft a distance of 319 feet (95.7 metres) at an altitude of 10 feet (3
metres), becoming the first Canuck to fly an airplane. But because the
flight took place in the United States, Baldwin was left out of the
limelight. On February 17, 1909,
his associate McCurdy flew
another biplane, the Silver Dart,
at Baddeck and became the first
Canadian to fly an airplane in
Canada. McCurdy received all
the attention and Baldwin was
left in obscurity.

In the 1920s and 1930s,
Baldwin developed hydrofoils
and entered politics, sitting for
four years in the Nova Scotia
legislature.

**Canadian aviation pioneers
Casey Baldwin (left) and John
McCurdy (right) at Baddeck,
Nova Scotia.**

[NAC/PA89117]

QUESTION?

Was the woman who inspired the Broadway musical The King and I *from Canada?*

ANSWER.

Anna Leonowens was born Anna Crawford in Wales and travelled around the world, but she spent most of the last years of her life in Canada and died in Montreal in 1915.

Anna, who was later immortalized in the book *Anna and the King of Siam*, which was subsequently turned into the popular Broadway musical and movie *The King and I*, was born in 1834 and spent some of her youth living in India. She married a British officer, Thomas Leonowens, in 1851 and moved with him to Singapore, where he was stationed in 1856. When he died a few years later after an all-day tiger hunt, Anna received an invitation to teach the royal children in Siam (now Thailand).

She and her son arrived in Bangkok in 1862 and stayed there until 1867. She became quite a prominent citizen, but after five years decided she and her family needed a better climate for health reasons. The family moved back to England, and with the children in boarding school, she went on to the United States. Leonowens wrote about her experiences in two books, *The English Governess* and *The Romance of the Harem*, and became much in demand as a lecturer in the United States. Her daughter married a Scottish banker, Thomas Fyshe, and went to live in Halifax. Leonowens joined them sometime around 1880, although one source says she moved to Halifax in 1876.

During her Halifax years, Leonowens organized a book club, a Shakespearean society, and was founding secretary of the Halifax Council of Women. She also helped start the arts university there. One source reports she left Halifax in 1897 to move to Germany, but her obituary in the Montreal *Gazette* indicates she moved to Montreal that year to join the Fyshe family. During her years in Montreal, Leonowens was at one time president of the Baby and Foundling Hospital. She was living on McTavish Street in Montreal when she died in January 1915. Her obituary described her as "a woman whom it was a privilege to know."

QUESTION?   *Who took the first photographs of Canada?*

ANSWER.   Although we can't be 100 per cent sure that someone didn't just take a camera outside one day and snap some shots, it's likely the first person was British metallurgist and scientist Hugh Lee Pattinson. According to information from the George Eastman House: International Museum of Photography and Film in Rochester, New York, Pattinson took the first photos in Canada during a visit to Niagara Falls.

Pattinson was on a business trip in April 1840 to examine the status of mineral rights in the area. He decided to make a side trip to see Niagara Falls and took several daguerreotypes (an early form of photograph) while there. Because he was also the first amateur photographer to take shots of the site, the museum claims he is the one who set the precedent for tourists to take such shots of the Falls, a tradition that continues to this day. Some of Pattinson's photographs were displayed at the museum in the summer of 1997.

QUESTION?

Who was the Canadian who started the Fuller Brush Company?

ANSWER.

The man who founded the company that became famous for selling brushes door to door was Alfred Fuller of Nova Scotia. Although Fuller described himself as something of "a country bumpkin" when he went into business, he eventually built a company that generates millions of dollars in sales annually today.

Fuller, one of twelve children, was born on January 13, 1885, in Welsford, situated in Nova Scotia's Annapolis Valley. The Fullers lived on a seventy-five-acre farm and Alfred, nicknamed "Uppie" as a child, worked there until he left home at eighteen. He moved to the Boston area, where some of his brothers and sisters lived. The only advice he received from his father was to be thrifty, save money, and live cleanly.

Fuller worked as a trolley conductor, got fired, and then held other jobs from which he was fired — even one time by his brother. He eventually got work selling brushes door to door for a company, and after about a year he decided he could do better on his own. His parents initially opposed the idea, but when he returned to Nova Scotia to tell them about it a second time, they supported him.

Fuller started his company in the basement of his sister's house with $375 in savings and some ideas for brushes that his previous employers had rejected. After four months, in April 1906, he moved his operations to Hartford, Connecticut, and initially called the enterprise the Capitol Brush Company, inspired by the state capitol building there. As the company grew, he began expanding into other states and eventually into Canada.

By 1913, he hadn't yet registered the company name, so he took the opportunity to rename the firm the Fuller Brush Company. In 1919, the company recorded its first $1 million in annual sales. Today, the company's large manufacturing plant in Kansas offers a range of more than two thousand home and personal-care products. Fuller died in December 1973.

QUESTION?   *What is the Canadian connection to the three-quart milk jug?*

ANSWER.   Jan Verdun left his native Holland in 1930 to be a farm labourer in Canada and eventually bought a feed mill in the southwestern Ontario town of Aylmer, where he went on to design the world's first three-quart milk jug. Not only that, he was also the proprietor of Canada's first modern convenience store.

According to his son Bob, Verdun began to develop his entrepreneurial skills when he pedalled out of Toronto on his bicycle to sell pins, shoelaces and other goods to farmers as a way of paying for his degree from the Ontario Agricultural College in Guelph.

In 1942, after working for dairies and feed companies, he bought the feed mill in Aylmer. He later added a farm so he could breed Holstein cattle, which produced milk faster than it was being sold.

Verdun discovered the cash-and-carry milk business in the United States and asked himself why milk was still being delivered to Canadian homes daily in small bottles when it could be bought in larger quantities at lower prices.

Jan Verdun, inventor of the world's first three-quart milk jug.
[Photo: Bob Verdun]

He designed a three-quart milk jug, which was ideal for consumers, and built a dairy with a lunch counter and a small store for grocery staples.

The opening of the first milk convenience store in March 1956, however, almost turned sour. Aylmer town council didn't want to grant him a licence to sell milk because the town already had two dairies. So he cleverly suggested his business be restricted to store sales only.

Then the glass makers refused to break with the tradition of manufacturing only one-quart bottles or even smaller ones. Verdun threatened to import U.S. gallon containers before Dominion Glass finally agreed to make three-quart jugs.

Verdun's Dairy was an instant hit: Consumers warmed to the fact that they could buy an affordable week's supply of milk and other goods from 7 A.M. to 11 P.M., seven days a week. A long-running special in the late 1950s and early 1960s was a jug of milk and a pound of butter for one dollar.

Advancing technology soon led to the packaging of milk in plastic bags, and Verdun's Dairy was too small to compete. Eventually, Verdun's reign as Jug Milk King ended and he began importing and breeding Charolais beef cattle. He founded the Ontario Charolais Association. Verdun died on October 22, 1996, in St. Thomas, Ontario, at the age of eighty-six.

QUESTION?   *Which Canadian was one of the few black surgeons to participate in the U.S. Civil War?*

ANSWER.   The Canadian black surgeon Anderson Ruffin Abbott was a member of that select group. And while that is significant historically, Abbott has other claims to fame as well.

Around 1835, Abbott's family moved from the United States to Toronto where his father eventually became a thriving real estate broker, according to Dalyce Newby, an international student advisor and Intercultural Centre coordinator at Humber College who has written a book about Abbott's life.

Abbott, who was born in Toronto in 1837, was the first Canadian-born black to receive a license to practise medicine; he studied at the Toronto School of Medicine. In those days there were several proprietary schools, and a student could gain a license to practise either by taking a series of classes or by taking some classes and apprenticing under an experienced doctor. In Abbott's case, the mentor was Dr. A. T. Augusta. In addition to studying at the Toronto School of Medicine, Abbott took classes at the Buxton Mission School, the Toronto Academy at Knox College, and Oberlin College in Ohio. When the Civil War broke out, he sent a letter to Washington offering his medical services. He joined up with the help of Edwin Stanton, Secretary of War, after he passed the medical exam. Abbott ended up as a contract surgeon with the North, one of only eight black doctors who served in the Civil War.

Some sources report that Abbott became good friends with Abraham Lincoln and his family during this time. Newby, however, claims the degree of friendship with Lincoln is questionable. There is no mention of Abbott in Lincoln's writings, while other blacks of the time are mentioned.

But after Lincoln was assassinated, Mary Todd Lincoln did give Abbott the shawl the former president had worn to his first inauguration, in 1861. The Abbott family kept the shawl for many years before giving it to the American branch of the family. It's now housed in the Wisconsin State Historical Society's textile collection.

After the war, in 1871, Abbott moved to Chatham, Ontario. From Chatham he moved to Dundas, then to Oakville, to Toronto, and after that to Chicago. He was active in civil and educational positions in the various cities where he lived. He was also an editor of journals and submitted articles to various papers. In 1894 he became administrator at Provident Hospital of Chicago, which was established by Hale Williams, the first black person or doctor ever to successfully perform open heart surgery. Abbott resigned from Provident in 1897.

He returned to Canada at the turn of the century and helped edit the *Missionary Messenger* of the Methodist Church. He died in 1913 and is buried in Toronto Necropolis and Crematorium, where his father had purchased a family plot. A few years ago, a musical about Abbott's life was performed in Toronto.

QUESTION?

*What is the story behind Sydney Guilaroff,
the Canadian who was known as the
"hairdresser to the stars"?*

ANSWER.

Guilaroff grew up in Winnipeg and Montreal and at age fourteen, left for New York, where he landed a job sweeping floors in a hair salon. He quickly learned the hairstyling trade and soon became "Mr. Sydney," at Antoine's, one of the Big Apple's finest salons. Not bad for a kid whose dad was hoping he'd grow up to be a shoe salesman.

Guilaroff's reputation with crimps and curls spread fast. Joan Crawford made him her pet stylist, and when he gave actress Claudette Colbert her first bangs, he gained national attention and was soon off to Hollywood, where he joined Metro-Goldwyn Mayer. At MGM he became known as "the man with the golden shears." As MGM's top stylist from 1934 until the late 1970s, he worked on more than twelve hundred motion picture sets.

He dyed Lucille Ball's hair fiery red and handled the coiffures for Crawford and Bette Davis in *Whatever Happened to Baby Jane*. On Grace Kelly's wedding day, Mr. Guilaroff was flown to Monaco with styling wand in hand, in case of emergency. When Michael Todd, Elizabeth Taylor's third husband, died in a plane crash, Guilaroff was at the foot of her bed consoling the star he first primped in the movie *National Velvet*. He once proposed to Greta Garbo after a lengthy affair, but was rebuffed and never spoke to her again.

Guilaroff, who never married, made headlines for more than his hairdressing skills. In 1938, he became the first single man in history to adopt a son, whom he named Jon, after Joan Crawford. The state of California had tried to stop the adoption but Guilaroff won out when he proved to a judge that he was both fit to be a parent and more moral than most other people. Eventually he adopted a second son and years later he adopted a former employee named Jose.

Guilaroff, who was born in England in 1907, died of pneumonia on May 28, 1997, in Beverly Hills, California, at age eighty-nine.

QUESTION?   *Who was frontiersman Jerry Potts, the man some call "Canada's Davy Crockett"?*

ANSWER.   In a 1980 biography, author D. Bruce Sealey describes Jerry Potts as one of the "last and greatest frontiersmen of Canada's Wild West ... one of the great builders of Canada." He won such praise because of his unique abilities as a go-between and conciliator in the 1800s, when conflict between Indians and settlers and the ravages of whiskey were combining to wreak havoc on the West.

Potts was born around 1840 in Montana, where his Scottish father was a clerk at a fur-trading post. His mother was a Native American, belonging to the Blood tribe of the Blackfoot Confederacy. He grew up in white settlements and, after his father was murdered in a case of mistaken identity, he lived among his mother's people. He split his time between Fort Benton, Montana, and southern Alberta, working as a hunter, wrangler, guide and fur trader.

Some say Jerry Potts was Canada's Davy Crockett.
[NAC/C69978]

A little man with rounded shoulders and a stunted growth of whiskers, he was known as one of the finest scouts, guides and interpreters in the West. He fought in many tribal wars and is said to have taken as many as nineteen scalps in one confrontation. Legend has it that he refused to have a gun pellet removed from his left ear lobe because he had earned it in battle and felt it brought him good luck. In 1874, at a time when the illegal whiskey trade was making a mockery of law and order in Canada's West, Potts was hired to lead the newly formed North West Mounted Police to capture Fort Whoop-Up, a bastion of whiskey traders. The fort was easily captured, but unfortunately the Americans had received advance warning and escaped with their whiskey before the Mounties arrived.

Nevertheless, the mission enhanced Potts's reputation as an ace guide, writes Sealey. Shortly after, he led the Mounties to a site which would later become Fort Macleod. Potts guided the Mounties for twenty-two years, earning a name for himself over time, often for his drinking prowess as much as his guiding abilities. It's been said that after drinking, Potts and a buddy would often try to trim their moustaches with six-shooters, facing each other at twenty-five paces.

For a while, Potts lived in a teepee outside Fort Macleod where he once had four wives at the same time, two of whom were sisters. Despite his reputation, Potts was a valuable asset to the Mounties. He spoke the languages of several tribes and was instrumental in building trust between Native people and the scarlet-coated mounted police. He also played a key role in the negotiation of treaties between Native people and the Canadian government.

Colonel Sam Steele, one of the most distinguished officers ever to serve with the force, once described Potts as "the man who trained the best scouts in the force ... as a scout and guide I have never met his equal ... it would take a large volume to describe even a small part of the usefulness of this man."

Potts died of tuberculosis on July 14, 1896. He was buried with full military honours in an RCMP cemetery in Fort Macleod, Alberta. As for the pellet in his ear — the one he felt brought him good luck? Well, he may have been right about its value, because he died a few months after the bullet worked its way out of his ear.

Following his death, the *Macleod Gazette* had this to say in a July 17, 1896, editorial: "For years he stood between the police on one side and his natural friends the Indians on the other and his influence always made for peace. Jerry Potts is dead but his name lives and will live."

Music
Lovers
Take
Note

A standing ovation for big-name homegrown stars like Alanis Morissette, The Guess Who, Bryan Adams, and Joni Mitchell; they've helped put Canadian music on the map — big time.

But in the following pages we also look at the other side of the country's music scene — the "B" side, if you will — a part of our musical heritage that has not made it into the spotlight, at least not for very long.

There's the Canadian pop band that filmed one of the first music videos ever — in 1964. The Canadian who wrote Malyasia's national anthem, as well as a hit song heard across the land during Canada's one hundredth birthday celebrations. And what about the Toronto band that posed nude or the group that used members of the Tonight Show Band to record one of its biggest hits?

Flip the page for a brief trip down Canadian music's memory lane.

QUESTION?

Is it true that band members from "The Tonight Show" played on a number-one Canadian record?

ANSWER.

"Gaslight" was the biggest hit for the Ugly Ducklings, a Toronto-based 1960s rock band. Just before the group split up in December 1967 it recorded the song, backed by a seventeen-piece band which included eleven musicians from "The Tonight Show."

Lead singer Dave Bingham says the Ugly Ducklings' record company wanted the band to use other musicians on the record in order to give it a better chance of getting a U.S. record deal. At first the band refused, but later, when Bingham was in New York City recording jingles, he was shown the song in a recording studio and couldn't resist.

The song was written by a New York cab driver and contained no input from other members of the Ugly Ducklings. It became the group's biggest single, reaching the number one spot in parts of Canada and selling about twenty-five thousand copies.

The Ugly Ducklings had been formed in Toronto in March 1965 and had quickly developed a reputation as one of the city's best "garage bands," so named because of the poor quality of their recordings. Their raunchy sound produced several early hits including "Nothin'," "She Ain't No Use to Me" and "Just in Case You Wonder," with its blistering lead-guitar solo. The band reunited for several concerts in the 1980s.

QUESTION?   *What Canadian band declined to perform at the Woodstock Festival in 1969?*

ANSWER.   It probably wasn't the greatest of career moves, but Lighthouse, the rock orchestra that was one of the most highly acclaimed and successful bands this country has ever produced, has the distinction of having declined to play at Woodstock in 1969.

Lighthouse, formed by Skip Prokop and Paul Hoffert, toured across Canada, had some success south of the border, and played at the Isle of Wight Festival, but it turned down Woodstock. The band had heard that the water was going to be spiked with drugs and that few security precautions were being taken. Band member Grant Fullerton, who played bass and sang in Lighthouse for awhile, remembers the decision with regret.

"We were booked to play Woodstock [in 1969], but our manager decided to pull us out of it because he thought it was going to be a bad scene. You look at it [now] and say, 'Boy that was certainly a bad mistake.'"

Fullerton left the band after a couple of years because of conflicts with the manager and the extreme pressure on Lighthouse. The band, with some of the original members such as Prokop, reunited in the 1990s and have released CDs.

QUESTION?   *Did Bobby Gimby, the man who wrote "Ca-na-da," do anything else of note?*

ANSWER.   The "Pied Piper of Canada" can also lay claim to having written the national anthem of Malaysia.

Bobby Gimby wrote the hit song "Ca-na-da" in 1967 as a way of celebrating Canada's one hundredth birthday. But it wasn't his first foray into nationalistic songs. When he was working in England in the early 1960s, the Vancouver-born musician was commissioned to write a song commemorating Malaysia's founding. The result was "Malaysia Forever."

As for his Canadian hit song, Gimby remembers that when he first played it for the Canada Centennial Commission, the members were less than enthusiastic.

He managed to convince them of its merits, and by the middle of that year people across the country were singing it. In the late 1980s, "Ca-na-da" was used by Canadian musicians lobbying the federal government as a symbol of how low the royalty rates for songs are in this country.

Gimby began performing music in the 1940s and continued to do so through the 1980s with school groups in Ontario.

QUESTION?

Which Canadian musician has won the most Juno Awards over the years? My bet's on Gordon Lightfoot.

ANSWER.

Close, but no cigar. Lightfoot has had a distinguished career in music over the past thirty-five years, picking up seventeen awards along the way, but that is only good enough for second place on the all-time biggest winner list. First place goes to singer Anne Murray, reports a spokesperson for the Canadian Academy of Recording Arts and Sciences (CARAS), which oversees the awards.

Murray had won twenty-five awards as of 1997 dating back to the 1960s, when they were called the Maple Leaf Awards. The name was changed to Junos in 1971, in part after the Roman goddess and in part to honour Pierre Juneau, one of the people responsible for instituting the Canadian-content rule for radio stations.

Murray, who has also won Grammy Awards, has won in a number of Juno categories, including album of the year, best female vocalist, best single, best children's recording, and as best female country vocalist.

And for all you Bryan Adams or Céline Dion fans out there, your favourites have each garnered fourteen Junos and one international achievement award as of the start of 1998, thus ranking third on the all-time list.

QUESTION? *What can you tell me about the album that was recorded in the 1960s by Canadian actor William Shatner of "Star Trek" fame?*

ANSWER. You may want Scotty to beam you out of here when you start listening to Shatner's 1968 album, *The Transformed Man*. To accompanying music, the Montreal-born Shatner lends his vocal "talents" to reciting such songs as "Mr. Tambourine Man," "It Was A Very Good Year," and "Lucy In The Sky With Diamonds." If you've ever wondered what it's like to be stunned by one of those phasers the "Star Trek" crew carries around, try listening to *The Transformed Man*.

The album got its start when Shatner met a producer named Cliff Ralke while they were both working on "Star Trek." It was Ralke's father, Don, who arranged and conducted the music on this album. Most of the album tracks consist of an instrumental piece followed by a Shatner recital.

William Shatner's recording, *The Transformed Man*, is not one of the high points in Canadian music history. [Photo: Catherine Blake]

Don Ralke wrote that "the idea of grouping the numbers in pairs is to unfold multiple perspectives of the same subject, like the two sides of a coin, tension and resolution." So for example, the third track, which has a musical piece called "Hamlet" followed by Shatner reciting "It Was A Very Good Year," was supposed to represent "a desire for death" and "the joy of living." Yeah, right. In the liner notes that accompanied the original album, Shatner wrote that he did the recording because "the roots go all the way back to my childhood in Canada. I remember going to the theatre and how I was always thrilled by the overture … Later, when I went to McGill University, I became very active in musical plays as a producer, actor, writer. So you see, music and I are old, familiar friends." And later in the notes he wrote, "The thrill I got from hearing this album all the way through was deeper and more satisfying than anything I have ever experienced."

A couple of cuts from the album have been featured on the Golden Throats CDs, which are selections of rock oddities put out by Rhino Records, and the album in its entirety has since been reissued on CD by Varèse Sarabande Records Incorporated of California.

QUESTION?   *What Canadian singer tried to sell his Juno
Award at a garage sale?*

ANSWER.   Singer-songwriter David Bradstreet won a
Juno Award as Most Promising Male Vocalist
back in the mid-seventies, but by 1982 he
had become disenchanted with the business
and had strained his vocal chords trying to
front a band sound that wasn't suited to his
gentle baritone.

Although Bradstreet maintains he was glad to win the Juno shortly
after the release of his first album, it put pressures on him that were
difficult to handle. He even half-jokingly tried to sell the award at a
garage sale, but the $15,000 price tag he put on it discouraged buyers,
he told us with a laugh.

Bradstreet was one of the most popular and successful performers on
the folk-music scene through the 1970s. Among his most successful
songs during his performing career were "Renaissance" (with which
Valdy had a hit), and the single "Long, Long Road." In the mid-eighties,
he started using his home studio to compose industrial film scores and
commercials for the likes of Xerox, Radio Shack, and the Canada
Winter Games. He began performing again in the nineties.

QUESTION?

What Canadian rock band was involved in Canada's first professional pop music video?

 ANSWER.

The video you speak of is a film that shows Ottawa band The Esquires performing two songs, "Man from Adano" and "Gee Whiz It's You." The footage was filmed in 1964 for use in a novelty jukebox.

Esquires' drummer Richard Patterson told us that the video was made to be viewed in jukeboxes brought from Europe by Ottawa entrepreneur Mac Levin. When a music selection was made, a film showing the band performing would appear on a television-like screen built into the jukebox.

The Esquires made it onto the video when Levin discovered that most of the filmed performances in his jukeboxes were in Italian and French. He Canadianized his footage by filming the Esquires as they performed in a downtown Ottawa warehouse, not far from Parliament Hill.

Ottawa group The Esquires, in Canada's first professional pop-music video.

[Photo: The Collection of Richard Patterson]

Music buffs who put some change into the jukebox saw the Esquires playing "Man from Adano" in an Italian wine garden. Halfway through the song an attractive woman sits down and begins snapping her fingers to the music. The video for "Gee Whiz It's You" begins with a girl standing at a jukebox. As soon as she makes a selection, the Esquires appear on the screen and begin performing the song on a rock-and-roll stage. During the video lead singer Bob Harrington dances with the girl. Also performing on the video are Esquires' lead guitarist Gary Comeau; rhythm guitarist Paul Huot; bassist Clint Hierlihy and Patterson on drums.

The video jukeboxes were located in bars and restaurants in Ottawa and Cornwall and in neighbouring Quebec until the mid-1970s when most broke down and were scrapped. The Esquires video went missing until the late eighties, when versions of it were unearthed in an army trunk which survived a fire in Levin's Ottawa jukebox warehouse.

The film was repaired by Crawley Films of Ottawa, then transferred to a video-tape format by the National Archives' Sound and Vision Department in Ottawa. The original film has been part of the collection at the National Archives since 1987. Both videos have been aired in Canada on television stations MuchMusic and Bravo.

The Esquires formed in 1962 as Canada's answer to British band Cliff Richard and the Shadows. They released seven singles and one album and were the first Canadian pop group signed to the influential Capitol Records EMI Music Limited record label. In 1964 the group won the first RPM music award (precursor to today's Juno Awards) for top vocal and instrumental group of the year. The Esquires disbanded in the late 1960s, with members going on to play in a variety of bands and launch solo careers.

QUESTION?

What was Canada's musical connection to once-popular television sitcom "The Beverly Hillbillies?"

ANSWER.

Fans of the mid-sixties music scene probably remember Canadian singer Lucille Starr for her hit tune "The French Song," which, since its release in 1964, has reputedly sold more than seven million records and earned the singer one platinum and five gold records.

But Starr (real name Lucille Savoie), a native of St. Boniface, Manitoba, who was raised in Mallardville, British Columbia, and Windsor, Ontario, also appeared on a handful of TV shows in the 1970s and 1980s. At one point, she handled behind-the-scenes yodelling for Beverly Hillbillies character Cousin Pearl.

As a singer, she and her former husband Bob Regan, who also sang, toured Canada for twenty years as the Canadian Sweethearts before moving to California and linking up with A & M Records, which was run by Herb Alpert and Gerry Moss. She re-recorded her earlier 1950s version of "The French Song" and the bilingual tune, with musical backup from Alpert's band The Tijuana Brass, soared to international fame. The song earned her tours in South Africa, Australia and Holland.

It was following a seven-year break from the music business in the early 1970s that she supplied Cousin Pearl's yodelling voice. When we found Starr, she was living in Nashville and was still touring.

QUESTION?

Was a Canadian group responsible for the song considered to be the first rock 'n' roll hit?

ANSWER.

In the early 1950s, the stars of pop music were singers such as Frank Sinatra, Vic Damone, Patti Page and Perry Como. Rock 'n' roll was still undefined and waiting for a young man in Memphis named Elvis Presley to push it into the spotlight.

But a prototype of rock 'n' roll was being developed by black musicians such as Fats Domino, Chuck Willis and Johnny Otis. Back then, the two different poles of pop music were coloured black and white.

A Canadian quartet, who left the choir loft of Toronto's St. Michael's Cathedral, played gigs around Ontario and eventually made it to the recording studios of New York, contributed much to the blending of big-band swing and rhythm and blues that would become rock 'n' roll.

The group was the Crew-Cuts, and in some circles their song "Sh-Boom" is considered to be the first rock 'n' roll hit. To many critics the Crew-Cuts were just another vocal act doing covers of so-called "black songs" and reaping the benefits. But it was only after the group recorded the Chords' song "Sh-Boom" that it became a number-one hit.

The quartet's Rudi Maugeri has this opinion: "If we hadn't done 'Sh-Boom,' [it] would not have become a major hit," he said. "If we hadn't done 'Don't Be Angry' or 'Ko Ko Mo (I Love You So)' or 'Earth Angel,' these songs would not have helped the black groups get their music to the white masses. They helped us by writing good material, and we helped them by doing their material and presenting it to white audiences.

"You see, you couldn't have gone completely from big band to rock 'n' roll without a group like ours to mesh it together. It couldn't have gone from Harry James to Elvis Presley."

Other Crew-Cuts Pat Barrett and John Perkins (his brother Ray was the fourth member) agree, saying that their recordings created new audiences for black material. The Crew-Cuts were named to the Canadian Music Hall of Fame in 1984.

QUESTION? *What Canadian rock group posed nude in the early seventies to promote their album?*

ANSWER. About twenty-five years ago, a saying in Toronto pop-music circles went like this: "Lighthouse plays for peace; Fludd plays for chicks."

That may help explain how the Toronto-based Fludd came to bare all when promoting an album. Their wild antics, such as posing nude for the now-defunct *Rainbow* magazine and dressing up flamboyantly with glitter, make-up and tight pants, often got Fludd into trouble. They were banned from playing at several venues.

Ed Pilling, who led the group with his late brother Brian, recalls the nude photo fondly.

"I guess we were pretty cheeky back then. One of the things we tried to do was shake up the bag. The Toronto scene was very dull. There's nothing wrong with a bit of controversy if you don't do anything bad."

The controversy was fueled when the band wanted to call its first album "Cock On," a British euphemism for "right on." The record company and distributors balked at the idea.

Pilling says the band members were upset and decided to pose for the nude picture as a kind of tongue-in-cheek (pardon the pun) protest. They included the picture in a promo package when they officially released the album one night at Toronto's Inn on the Park. They didn't stop there: Fludd also got into trouble when one of their later albums, *Great Expectations*, featured a pregnant woman's stomach on the cover.

Nevertheless, Fludd managed to rise above its sex-charged image to record a number of successful songs in the first half of the seventies, such as "Turned 21," "Brother and Me," and the laid-back country-flavoured "Cousin Mary."

QUESTION?   *How did Canadian band A Foot in Coldwater get its name?*

ANSWER.   The band, which got started in a farmhouse in Brougham, Ontario, northeast of Toronto, took its name from a term that in its euphemistic sense means you've made a wrong turn. In other words, you're in deep shit.

The band members were Paul Naumann, Danny Taylor, Alex Machin, Hughie Leggat and Bob Horne, and the group is best known for its classic piece of Canadian rock, the hit single "Make Me Do Anything You Want."

A Foot in Coldwater evolved out of Toronto bands The Lords of London, which later became Nucleus, and the group Island. Shortly after they began practising in the Brougham farmhouse, they scored their big hit, which was written by Taylor and Naumann.

"There was a freshness to ['Make Me Do Anything You Want']," said vocalist Alex Machin. "But that song wasn't even very representative of the way the band sounded. We were a much heavier band than that song." The group reunited in the eighties for some concerts.

QUESTION? *Which Canadian band had one of the best selling singles ever in Japan?*

ANSWER. The honour goes to the Montreal group Mashmakhan and their number-one single "As The Years Go By." Not only did it rocket to the top of Canadian charts in 1970, it went on to become one of the best selling singles ever in Japan.

"I wasn't surprised," said Pierre Senecal, Mashmakhan's keyboard player. "I remember when I wrote that song I felt I had something that was extremely commercial. It's one of those songs that took me fifteen minutes to write."

The song broke first in Montreal, before climbing charts around the world (it also hit number thirty-one on Billboard). Guitarist Rayburn Blake described it as "a little tongue-in-cheek thing at the end of a long melodramatic piece we were playing [in the studio] — we were getting a little heavy even for us.

"People remember it who were much younger than I was at the time — people eight or nine years old. And that's a good feeling. I'm not going to knock that."

And as for the group's name, it comes from a plant that grows in Bermuda, called by the locals "match-me-if-you-can."

QUESTION?

What Canadian folksinger once taught Paul Peterson of the television program "The Donna Reed Show" how to sing?

ANSWER.

Ken Tobias, whose hits included "Every Bit Of Love," "Dream Number Two," "Run Away With Me," and "Fly Me High," was the vocal instructor. Righteous Brother Bill Medley caught Tobias's act early on and was impressed enough to take him to Hollywood. While there, the Canadian singer-songwriter hung out with actor Dack Rambo (who went on to star in "Dallas") and helped Peterson of "The Donna Reed Show" with his singing.

Tobias, a former Maritimer who sang "I just want to make music all night long" was still involved in the music scene in the nineties writing film and television scores, and his songs are still played on radio stations across Canada.

QUESTION?   *Canadians Céline Dion and Alanis Morissette have done well at the Grammy Awards in recent years. What other Canadians have won?*

ANSWER.   Dion and Morissette were certainly not the first Canadians to grab a Grammy, the award given out each year by the National Academy of Recording Arts and Sciences for excellence in music. Rocker Bryan Adams, for example, has been on the podium in the past, but you can go back much further than that to see Canadian successes.

Percy Faith won Record of the Year in 1960 with the "Theme From A Summer Place" while Gale Garnet won a Grammy for best folk performance in 1964 for her hit "We'll Sing In the Sunshine." Anne Murray received her first award in 1974 and won a few other times since.

Oscar Peterson has won several times in various jazz categories; he even won three years in a row, from 1977 to 1979.

But David Foster, formerly of British Columbia, has garnered the most awards over the years. The producer/songwriter has been nominated thirty-eight times since 1979 and had won fourteen Grammies and a President's Merit award by 1998. He's picked up Grammies for his work on such albums as Céline Dion's *Falling Into You*, the soundtrack for *The Bodyguard*, Natalie Cole's single "Unforgettable," and the Dreamgirls' Broadway cast album. Foster was chosen producer of the year in 1984.

QUESTION?   *What Canadian group was known as the "heaviest band in the world?"*

ANSWER.   Thundermug was their name and their trademark was sheer power — lots of it. Their performances often provoked noise complaints, and their lead guitarist once declared the band intended to be the loudest group in Canada.

They were an early-1970s heavy-metal band, formed in the London, Ontario area and if critical reaction was any indication, they may well have succeeded — reviewers were known to leave Thundermug's concerts early, with their hands clutching their ears. The group's music was so loud that rehearsing was often a problem. They would practise with other bands, including Rush and The Stampeders, but their high-decibel level often meant others practising nearby had to take a break until Thundermug finished. Evolving out of bands The Ookpiks, The Village Guild, The Soul Agents, Pink Orange, Bodmas and The Testament, they were once referred to as London's answer to Led Zeppelin.

"Our trademark was certainly noise," lead vocalist Joe De Angelis of Belmont, Ontario, near London, said in an interview. "We were constantly getting in trouble; we were too loud for most clubs. It was a constant battle." Other members of the original band were guitarist Bill Durst, bassist Jim Corbett and drummer Ed Pranskus.

Their hits included "Africa" and "Orbit" and they released four albums. Some members of the band reunited in the early 1990s; they have recorded and achieved moderate success with several new songs — none of which were as ear-shattering as the original band's tunes.

Our
Political
Agenda

Not all good political questions are raised in Question Period. We've dug up a few that will keep you debating the merits of our political system and its workings for longer than any backbench MP will ever rant. Women as political pioneers, parliamentary pages, and election escapades are all part of this chapter.

And in case you want to know how far underground politicians would have gone if the heat (of the nuclear kind) had been turned up, read on.

QUESTION?

Who held the office of prime minister for the shortest period of time? Who has been PM the longest?

ANSWER.

Many Canadians think Kim Campbell, or maybe Joe Clark, held the PM's job for the shortest period of time but that's not true. The PM with the shortest stay in office was Sir Charles Tupper, a Conservative who led the country for just 69 days in 1896. He was replaced by Liberal Sir Wilfrid Laurier in an election fought over the explosive issue of public funding for Catholic schools in Manitoba. Tupper was Canada's sixth prime minister.

Others who barely had time to get a feel for the PM's office include John Turner, who was prime minister for 80 days in 1984 before his Liberals were defeated by the surging popularity of Brian Mulroney and his Conservatives. The next shortest stay in office was that of Conservative PM Arthur Meighen, who, in 1926, during his second stint as PM, lasted just 89 days before being tossed out by the Liberals under William Lyon Mackenzie King.

In October 1993, Campbell's Conservatives lost to Prime Minister Jean Chrétien's Liberals after she had been PM for 135 days. Clark, also a Conservative, held office for 273 days in 1979–80 before losing to Pierre Trudeau.

The prime minister who led the country for the longest period of time was Mackenzie King, who was PM for nearly twenty-two years over three separate terms of office, 1921 to 1926, 1926 to 1930 and 1935 to 1948, when he fell to the Liberals, led by Louis St. Laurent.

The record for the longest unbroken tenure as PM goes to Sir Wilfrid Laurier, who held office for more than fifteen years straight, from July 1896 until October 1911. Laurier was PM for four consecutive terms, 1896 to 1900, 1900 to 1904, 1904 to 1908 and 1908 to 1911, when he was defeated by Robert Borden's Conservatives over the issue of free trade with the United States.

QUESTION?   *Where in Canada did women first have the legal right to vote?*

 ANSWER.   The honour goes to Manitoba, where females won the right to vote provincially in January 1916. At the same time, Manitoba granted women the right to stand for office. Saskatchewan followed suit, granting both rights less than two months later. The right to vote federally wasn't granted to women until 1918. In the election of 1917, however, female nurses in the armed forces, women with close relatives overseas fighting the war, and some women with property were allowed to vote.

But Quebec can also lay claim to this honour. Although Quebec was the last to give women the vote provincially, which it did in 1940, it was the first to grant the franchise, in a sense. Women who owned property in Quebec between 1809 and 1849 were allowed to vote municipally.

QUESTION?

It seems that men have always dominated Canadian politics, but what can you tell me about an all-woman municipal council in eastern Ontario back in 1967? And what are some other political firsts for women?

ANSWER.

Tweed, Ontario, a village in Hastings County east of Peterborough, has the distinction of being the first municipality in Canada to be governed by a woman reeve and four female councillors. The all-woman council catapulted the village into the spotlight in 1967, when provincial and national media took an interest in the unique group sitting around the table in Tweed's council chambers.

The council consisted of Reeve Barbara Allen and councillors Bosley, Courneyea, Sinclair, and Whitfield. It should be noted, however, that the five women weren't elected to council en bloc. Allen, Bosley and Courneyea received the nod from voters in the December 1966 election, but Sinclair and Whitfield didn't join council until 1967. Both became councillors following the resignations of two male council members who had been elected in December but left to pursue other interests.

Tweed's all-woman council lasted for only one term. In the next election Whitfield lost to a man by a narrow margin.

A number of other women have also been thrust into the public eye by virtue of election victories or political appointments. Louise McKinney made headlines on December 17, 1917, when she became the first woman in Canada to be elected to a provincial legislature, in Alberta; on December 6, 1921, Agnes Campbell MacPhail was the first woman to be elected to the House of Commons, when she won the Ontario riding of Grey South East in the first election where women had the right to vote; in 1930, Cairine Reay Wilson was the first female appointed to Canada's Senate and on October 15, 1936, Mary Teresa Sullivan was sworn in as a member of Halifax city council, the first female alderman in Canada.

On June 21, 1957, Ontario MP Ellen Loucks Fairclough, a native of Hamilton, Ontario, was appointed secretary of state in the government of Prime Minister John Diefenbaker, thus being the first woman appointed to the federal Cabinet. Blanche Margaret Meagher of Halifax became Canada's first female ambassador on October 22, 1958, when she was appointed ambassador to Israel. Meagher later served as Canada's ambassador to Austria and Sweden.

QUESTION?

Seventeen of Canada's twenty prime ministers bear the title Right Honourable. Why not the other three?

ANSWER.

The three PMs without the title Right Honourable are Alexander Mackenzie, who held office from November 1873 until October 1878; Sir John Joseph Caldwell Abbott, who was PM from June 1891 to November 1892 and Sir Mackenzie Bowell, who held office from December 1894 until April 1896.

First, let's explain who is entitled to the appellation. As stated in the *Table of Titles To Be Used In Canada*, the only persons in Canada accorded it are past and present governors general, prime ministers and chief justices of the Supreme Court, as well as other distinguished Canadians who have made outstanding or invaluable contributions to national life in Canada.

That, of course, means former prime ministers such as John A. Macdonald, Brian Mulroney, Pierre Trudeau and Lester Pearson have the title, as do former governor general Ramon Hnatysyn and former supreme court chief justice Brian Dickson. Seven persons still alive at the time this book was written had received the Right Honourable title for their contributions to Canadian life: Martial Asselin, a Cabinet minister in the government of John Diefenbaker and also a former senator and lieutenant-governor in Quebec; Ellen L. Fairclough, who in the government of Diefenbaker became Canada's first female Cabinet minister; Francis Alvin George Hamilton, also a Cabinet minister under Diefenbaker; Donald Mazankowski, former deputy prime minister under Mulroney; and Robert Stanfield, a former leader of the federal Conservative party. Three other eminent Canadians who received the title but later died are: Jean-Luc Pépin, Paul Martin, Sr., and John Whitney Pickersgill, all distinguished Liberal Cabinet ministers.

Prior to 1967 all Canadian prime ministers were designated as Honourable by the Canadian Privy Council, a body established in the Constitution Act, 1867, to advise the Crown, reports a spokesperson for

Canadian Heritage Promotion, Ceremonial and Canadian Symbols Promotion in Hull, Quebec. The only way they could be accorded the title Right Honourable was if they were sworn into the British Privy Council and most were.

So why weren't Abbott, Bowell and Mackenzie accorded the title Right Honourable? Because Mackenzie didn't want any special honour and Abbott and Bowell were not in office long enough to be summoned to the British Privy Council, explains the Canadian Heritage spokesperson. As a result, all three men are styled "Honourable," the title that is given to all federal and provincial Cabinet ministers and Speakers of the House of Commons, among others. Former federal Cabinet ministers and lieutenant-governors keep the title for life.

Since 1967, the governor general has been entitled to the appellation Right Honourable for life, and since 1968 the title has been accorded to the prime minister and chief justice of the Supreme Court for life. In 1992, to mark the 125th anniversary of Confederation, on the advice of Mulroney, the title Right Honourable was granted to eminent Canadians. And in 1993, again on the advice of Mulroney, the title was granted to Mazankowski.

Canadian prime ministers without the title Right Honourable: (a) Alexander Mackenzie [NAC/PA25302] **(b) Sir John Joseph Caldwell Abbott** [NAC/C8094] **(c) Sir Mackenzie Bowell** [NAC/C8100]

QUESTION?

What is the significance of world leaders and dignitaries planting trees at Rideau Hall in Ottawa?

ANSWER.

The tree plantings at Rideau Hall, the Ottawa residence of Canada's governor general, are undertaken to commemorate visits by members of the royal family, heads of state, and certain dignitaries, to mark special anniversary dates and to commemorate the end of a governor general's mandate, affirms Rideau Hall spokesperson Kate McGregor.

At the end of 1997, eighty-eight ceremonial trees had been planted on the thirty-two-hectare grounds, which are located at 1 Sussex Drive, near the home of Canada's prime minister.

The tradition began in April 1906, when a red oak was planted by Prince Arthur of Connaught, son of a future governor general. Since then, three trees have been planted by Queen Elizabeth II, in 1951 (when she was The Princess Elizabeth) and in 1957 and 1977. Others have been sunk into the ground by King George VI, May 21, 1939; Queen Juliana of the Netherlands, April 22, 1952; presidents of the Philippines, Corazon Aquino, November 3, 1989, and Fidel V. Ramos, November 30, 1997; and six U.S. presidents, most recently Bill Clinton, on February 23, 1995. Clinton's tree is a sugar maple.

In many cases spouses of heads of state such as Nancy Reagan and Prince Philip have planted trees near those planted by their husbands or wives.

Trees have also been planted at Rideau Hall to mark other special occasions. In October 1979, a sugar maple was planted in honour of International Year of the Child, and the seventy-fifth anniversary of Boy Scouts Canada was commemorated on May 29, 1982, with the planting of a Norway Maple.

QUESTION? *What kind of jobs did our MPs have before being elected? Have any made names for themselves outside of politics?*

ANSWER. Before jumping into the fray at Parliament Hill, the men and women who represent the interests of Canadians in the House of Commons had a wide range of careers. Members elected in the June 1997 federal election, for instance, include people who have treated the sick, flown airplanes, farmed, reported the news, wired homes and represented lawbreakers in court.

By far the most frequently listed pre-political occupation for MPs sitting in the thirty-sixth Parliament is the legal profession. Library of Parliament data show that 36 MPs elected in 1997 were lawyers, including Prime Minister Jean Chrétien, Deputy PM Herb Gray, former Conservative Leader Jean Charest, British Columbia New Democrat Svend Robinson and Alberta Reform MP Diane Ablonczy. The legal profession has always been heavily represented in the Commons: In the previous Parliament 47 MPs were lawyers.

The next most common field of endeavour for MPs is the world of business. Thirty-two of the most recently elected crop of MPs are business persons or business executives, including London, Ontario, Liberal MP Joe Fontana, Quebec Conservative MP André Bachand and Conservative Gilles Bernier of New Brunswick. Before being voted into Parliament, 16 MPs were administrators, including Liberal Claudette Bradshaw of New Brunswick, Ontario Liberal MP Aileen Carroll and Bloc Québécois MP Pierre Brien. There are others with business-related careers: accountants (7), consultants (14) and insurance executives/agents (2).

There are also 14 professors, 7 medical doctors, 15 farmers, 4 clergypersons, 19 teachers, 2 electricians, 2 carpenters, a probation officer, a bush pilot, 10 former members of the media, a radio station operator, a printer, a bank manager, 3 contractors, a student, 2 police officers, one nurse, an economist and 10 MPs who were municipal politicians before voters sent them to Ottawa. Preston Manning, the

Leader of the Official Opposition and head of the Reform Party, is listed as a consultant and party leader.

If you're looking for MPs with celebrity status, or even positions of notoriety outside of their political lives, you'll have to go back a few years. The most notorious was Métis leader Louis Riel, who led the North-West Rebellion in 1885 and was hanged for treason on November 16 of that year in Regina. Riel was elected in an October 13, 1873 by-election as member for the riding of Provencher in Manitoba and he was re-elected twice in 1874. On February 25, 1875, he was unseated and declared an outlaw.

Leonard "Red" Kelly played in the National Hockey League between 1947 and 1967 with the Detroit Red Wings and Toronto Maple Leafs and later coached the Los Angeles Kings, Pittsburgh Penguins and the Leafs. In 1962, while playing for Toronto, he was elected as Liberal MP for the riding of York West in Ontario and he was re-elected in 1963. He bowed out of the political arena in 1965 when he found his dual career too strenuous.

Andrée Champagne was elected as a Conservative MP in 1984 in the riding of St-Hyacinthe and was re-elected in 1988. She also served as minister of youth and Deputy Speaker of the House of Commons. In the late 1950s and early 1960s, she played the role of beautiful blonde heroine Donalda Laloge, on the popular Quebec daytime drama TV show "Les belles histoires des pays d'en haut."

Phil Edmonston was elected MP for the Quebec riding of Chambly in a by-election on February 12, 1990. A consumer advocate and journalist, he made a name for himself as editor of books designed to inform automobile buyers and drivers. Thousands of his books, known as Lemon-Aid guides, have been sold.

Before entering politics, Otto Jelinek won the pairs title and a gold medal at the 1962 World Figure Skating Championships in Prague, skating in the pairs competition with his sister Maria. Otto and Maria later went on to great success at the Ice Capades. Jelinek first skated onto the floor of the Commons in 1972, when he was elected Conservative MP for the Ontario riding of Oakville-Milton. He was re-elected in 1974, 1979, 1980, 1984 and 1988 and during his political career held a number of Cabinet posts including that of minister of revenue and minister of supply and services.

QUESTION? *Did Sir John A. Macdonald have a son who was also a successful politician?*

ANSWER. Hugh John Macdonald, son of Canada's first prime minister, never won the fame of his famous father but did win considerable acclaim in politics and law.

A native of Kingston, Ontario, the younger Macdonald served in the Canadian militia three times and took up law, practising in Toronto until 1882, when he moved to Winnipeg.

In 1891, friends urged him to run for politics and he was elected as a Conservative with his father present when he took his oath of office. (Sir John A. was a Liberal Conservative, forerunner of the Progressive Conservative Party.)

History books indicate Hugh John found politics of little interest and resigned his seat in 1894. In 1896 he was persuaded to re-enter public life but fell victim to a sweep by the Liberal government led by Sir Wilfrid Laurier and returned to his law practice. In the late 1890s, the Manitoba Conservative party asked Macdonald to be its leader and in the provincial election of 1899, the party won easily with Macdonald leading it on a platform of prohibition of liquor sales.

However, when Macdonald took his platform promises seriously, the party began conniving to get rid of him and it eventually persuaded him to resign so he could tackle Liberal Clifford Sifton in a federal election. He lost to the powerful Grit and that was the end of his political career.

For services rendered to the Conservatives, Macdonald was appointed a police magistrate for Winnipeg and the federal party had him knighted in 1913. As a magistrate he was known as humane and always willing to give defendants ample time to explain their side of a case.

In 1927, as a result of circulatory troubles, he had one leg amputated, but in spite of his handicap, he continued to serve on the bench, being carried into court each day by two burly policemen. He died on March 29, 1929, and was accorded a state funeral.

QUESTION?   *Have Canadians always voted on the same day in federal general elections?*

 ANSWER. Since Confederation, the Canadian electorate has gone to the polls on the same day in all but two general elections, notes John Enright, spokesperson for Elections Canada in Ottawa.

In the first federal election in the history of the country, voters cast their ballots between August 7 and September 20, 1867. The winner — John A. Macdonald's Liberal Conservative Party — wasn't announced until September 24, about six weeks after the first ballots were cast. Canadians also voted on more than one day in Canada's second election, which took place between July 20 and October 12, 1872, and sent Liberal Alexander Mackenzie to the prime minister's office.

Both elections were spread over many weeks because distance and poor communications meant voters could not always make it to the voting booth on time. "In those days polls were taken to the nearest community but not to outlying areas. That meant voters had to travel to towns from up in the mountains or in the logging camps or mines where they worked. That could take days," explains Enright.

Once voters in one area had cast their ballots, the poll would be closed and ballot boxes were moved on to another village. In Pembroke, Ontario, north of Ottawa, for example, the ballot box would stay put for three days before moving on to the next community. By the time Canada's third election was held more polls had been set up in a wider area, making voting much more accessible to all voters. In 1874 the federal election was held on January 22 and, for the record, the same-day vote resulted in the defeat of Mackenzie and the return of Macdonald to the PM's office.

Since then every general election has been held on a single day, says Enright, although in the spring of 1997, when the Red River flooded, there was talk of changing the June 2 date of the election for Manitoba voters because the high water might have prevented some Manitobans from making it to the polls. However, a change in date was nixed because after visiting the disaster area Chief Electoral Officer Jean-Pierre Kingsley felt the situation was "not extreme enough" to warrant a delay in the vote, reports Enright.

The election could have been delayed in Manitoba by way of Article 13 of the Canada Elections Act, which gives the chief electoral officer power to delay an election if "by reason of a flood, fire, or other disaster it is impracticable" to hold an election in any electoral district.

QUESTION?   *How do young Canadians become pages at Parliament Hill? Is it true that there was once a height restriction?*

ANSWER.   House of Commons pages — the young people you see scurrying around the House of Commons in smart black-and-white suits when Parliament is in session — have served the Commons since Confederation, says program co-ordinator Roxanne Enman, a native of Victoria West, Prince Edward Island, who served as a page in 1990.

They work in the Commons Chamber to provide services to members of Parliament, such as photocopying, delivery of research material, answering phones, collecting speeches delivered by MPs and passing messages between members and their aides. They also deliver glasses of water to members whose throats dry out during long-winded addresses and they sometimes speak to youth groups whose members are interested in enrolling in the program.

The page program is open to graduating high-school students from across Canada who have been accepted by the University of Ottawa or Carleton University, in Ottawa, and the University of Hull, in Hull, Quebec, across the Ottawa River from the Nation's Capital. Candidates must be Canadian citizens, have a good knowledge of French and English and an average of at least 80 per cent when they graduate from high school. About four hundred young people apply for the job each year and interviews are conducted in the legislatures of the provinces or territories where they live. Pages are selected by the deputy principal clerk responsible for journals and the page program.

The 1997–98 program had forty pages — seventeen boys and twenty-three girls — with representation from all provinces and territories in Canada. Pages are paid $9,250 for a one-year stint from August to August and work about fifteen hours a week. On average, fourteen pages are on duty during the hours the House is sitting.

While the program is open to males and females from across Canada, it wasn't always that way. For many years after Confederation, it was customary for the House of Commons to choose only boys, often as young as eleven years old and only from poor families in the Ottawa-Hull area. And history informs us that Parliamentarians were concerned that boys taller than 5 feet 6 inches would block their view during debates, so tall boys were automatically out of the running.

That all changed, however, in the 1970s, after a study of the American page program was completed. In 1978, following the recommendations of a committee set up by Commons Speaker James Jerome, the program welcomed boys and girls of any height from across Canada. "The program became a living political science course as was the intention of Mr. Jerome," comments Enman, noting that many pages develop a lifelong interest in politics.

Through a separate program the Senate also employs pages to provide essentially the same services to senators.

Parliamentary pages (left to right): Erin Matheson, Montreal, Quebec; Trevor Tchir, St. Albert, Alberta; Chrystall Waddington, Surrey, British Columbia; and Jules Sisk, Fredericton, New Brunswick.

[Photo: Randy Ray]

QUESTION?

What can you tell me about a series of underground shelters built by the Canadian government during the Cold War years?

ANSWER.

Several bunkers were built in Canada between 1959 and 1967, each designed to ensure governments could continue to function in the event of nuclear attack.

The best known of these was the Diefenbunker, a four-storey subterranean office building near the village of Carp, twenty-five kilometres west of Ottawa. With a total area of 100,000 square feet, it was constructed to house top government officials and support staff if a nuclear bomb were dropped on or near Ottawa. High-level members of the team which would have operated the country from the bunker would have included the governor general, prime minister, the minister of external affairs, the minister of national defence and one additional minister appointed by the PM, says André Renault of Ottawa, who was one of the Emergency Preparedness Canada officials responsible for keeping all bunkers ready in case of a nuclear attack. Deputy ministers, directors general, assistant deputy ministers, radio broadcasters and technicians from various telecommunications agencies such as Bell Canada would also have been housed in the facility.

The bunker could accommodate about five hundred occupants for thirty days, until the fallout from an attack had dissipated, and also serve as a communications hub, which as it turned out, was its primary function throughout its thirty-three years of service. It was officially known as the Central Emergency Government Headquarters, and initially the government firmly maintained that the massive new structure was an army signals establishment, which was, in fact, a key function of the facility and an important reason why it had been built. When information about the bunker's real purpose leaked out, the media dubbed it the Diefenbunker after John Diefenbaker, the prime minister at the time.

Its layout included a hospital, bedrooms and offices for the governor general and prime minister, a Bank of Canada vault, a decontamination unit, a huge kitchen, and a cafeteria and a CBC radio studio to broadcast advice to the nation if Canada or the United States were ever threatened by nuclear radiation, according to Connie Higginson Murray, who is writing a book about the Cold War. It provided blast protection and was also protected against radioactive fallout.

A supporting telecommunications underground site, known as the Richardson Transmitter Facility, was located near Perth, a town about an hour west of Ottawa. It was a much smaller emergency facility which had been built to receive and relay electronic communications from the Diefenbunker and protect communications technicians who worked there. It provided a measure of protection against radioactive fallout but was not blastproof.

The Diefenbunker was decommissioned in 1994, when Canadian Forces Station Carp closed. In the same year it was declared a National Historic Site and the most important surviving Cold War site in Canada by the Historic Sites and Monument Board of Canada. The site is now owned by a non-profit group which sponsors public tours and was planning to open a Cold War museum at the site.

Six other bunkers, each having two storeys under the ground and known as Regional Emergency Government Headquarters, were built to serve as military communications centres and as emergency provincial-government facilities.

These shelters were in Nanaimo, at the Nanaimo Military Camp, on the southwest edge of the community; in Alberta at Canadian Forces Base Penhold, outside of Red Deer; in Manitoba at CFB Shilo between Winnipeg and Brandon; in Ontario at CFB Borden, one hundred kilometres north of Toronto; in Quebec at Camp Valcartier, on CFB Valcartier, thirty-two kilometres north of Quebec City and in Nova Scotia at Canadian Forces Station Debert, about twenty kilometres northwest of Truro. Each bunker could hold between 300 and 325 people. They could provide protection from radiation but were not made to be blastproof because they were located away from target centres, Renault said in an interview.

Other provincial-government emergency facilities, although not underground and not as well protected as the others, were located in Regina, in the basement of the Queens building in the city's downtown; in the basement of a federal building in Fredericton but later moved to an above-ground building at CFB Gagetown; in Charlottetown in the basement of the Dominion Building in the city's core and in St. John's in the Sir Humphrey Gilbert building in the city's downtown but later moved to a commercial shopping area on the outskirts of St. John's.

Like the Diefenbunker, all the emergency government facilities were closed in 1993–94, when it was decided the threat of nuclear war no longer existed. At the time this book was written, ambitious plans were in the works for some of the bunkers, including the Diefenbunker. At Debert, for example, the Colchester Park Development Society was hoping to use the shelter to train and house air cadets and also as a Cold War military museum.

QUESTION?

I understand it is against the law to use the name Parliament Hill for commercial purposes. How did this come about?

ANSWER.

The words Parliament Hill, when used together, are indeed protected in legislation. Use them to earn money, by starting a business named Parliament Hill Internet Service, for instance, and you could have the feds banging on your door asking for a name change. You could also face a fine and a jail term.

This protection is set out in federal legislation, specifically, *An Act respecting the use of the expression "Parliament Hill,"* which received royal assent on May 19, 1972.

According to House of Commons Debates obtained from the Library of Parliament, the legislation, originally known as Bill C-78, was the brainchild of George McIlraith, veteran Liberal MP for the riding of Ottawa Centre. It was drafted after McIlraith learned that an entrepreneur in Ottawa planned to open an establishment known as the Parliament Hill Hotel.

The bill was introduced as a Private Member's Bill on February 25, 1972, and was supported in the Commons by a number of MPs including Stanley Knowles, New Democratic Party MP for Winnipeg North Centre, and Donald MacInnis, Conservative MP for Cape Breton-East Richmond.

"As best I can ascertain, there has been no attempt to use this designation by any other enterprise in the first 102 years of Confederation ... It seems to me this is a most inappropriate designation as applied to anything other than this immediate area and grounds on which the Parliament Buildings are situated, and the name should be reserved for that purpose," McIlraith told the Commons after moving the bill for second reading.

"I am sure we all agree that the term 'Parliament Hill' has a certain meaning in this country and that we do not want to see it commercialized," added Knowles.

Since becoming law, the bill has prohibited anyone from using the term Parliament Hill in Canada — other than on the specific ground occupied by the Parliament Buildings — to describe a property, site, place or location that is a commercial establishment or provider of commercial services.

So forget naming your campground outside Regina "Parliament Hill Camping," or your music store in Fredericton "Parliament Hill Discount CDs," and don't even think of starting up "Parliament Hill Food Market," no matter where you live in Canada.

In addition, the name cannot be used in Canada to identify goods, merchandise, wares or articles for commercial use or for sale. So someone selling "Parliament Hill" cheeseburgers or "Parliament Hill" pizza in Vancouver, Montreal, Halifax, or any other Canadian community, would be breaking the law.

However, it's fine, according to an Ottawa lawyer we consulted, to sell Parliament Donuts or Parliament Tattoos anywhere in the country. And established products such as Parliament Cigarettes and HP Sauce, are not affected by the legislation.

If you are convicted of violating the Act, the maximum penalty is a fine of two thousand dollars and/or six months' imprisonment.

By the way, when the owner of the Ottawa hotel was informed that MPs felt use of the name Parliament Hill Hotel was inappropriate, the name was changed. Who says backbenchers wield little power?

Parliament Hill: Use of the name for business purposes is a no-no.

[NAC/PA34224]

QUESTION?

How much were MPs and the prime minister paid in the days of Confederation? How do their paycheques compare today?

ANSWER.

When Sir John A. Macdonald formed Canada's first government in 1867, members of Parliament were paid $6 per day and could earn a maximum of $600 a year. They were also paid 10 cents a mile for travel. It is not clear in documents obtained from the Library of Parliament whether Sir John A. earned extra pay for his duties as prime minister.

In 1873, MPs' pay rose to $10 per day, or a maximum of $1,000 per year, and the prime minister of the day was earning an extra $3,000 on top of his pay as an MP. By 1905, MPs were earning $20 a day and "no more" than $2,500 a year, according to the Library of Parliament, and were also compensated with an unspecified amount for moving or transportation expenses.

In 1945, MPs could earn a maximum of $4,000 per year. They also began receiving a non-taxable allowance of $2,000 per year to cover expenses. At this point, the prime minister was being paid an extra $15,000.

In 1963, MPs were earning $12,000 per annum, plus a $6,000 non-taxable allowance, and an unspecified amount for transportation, travel, and telecommunications expenses; the prime minister was earning $37,000 plus a $2,000 car allowance. In 1980 MPs were earning $30,600 per year, plus a non-taxable stipend for expenses ranging from $13,500 to $17,900, depending on where they lived. The prime minister was earning $68,400, plus his MP allowance and a $2,000 car expense allowance.

As of January 1, 1998, MPs were paid $64,400, plus a tax-free expense allowance of between $21,300 and $34,200, depending on where they lived, and the prime minister was earning $134,320, plus his MP allowance and a $2,000 car expense allowance.

MPs who were cabinet ministers were earning $111,045, plus their MP allowances and a $2,000 car allowance; the leader of the official opposition was paid $113,500, plus MP allowances and a $2,000 car allowance. The Commons Speaker is paid the same as the leader of the Opposition but receives a $3,000 car allowance and a $3,000 rent allowance.

Ordinary MPs can boost their salaries substantially by taking on other jobs. Members who are their parties' House leader can earn an extra $10,100 to $23,800; whips, who are responsible for ensuring MPs are in the House for votes and other important business, are paid between $7,500 and $13,200 extra; MPs who chair committees and those who are parliamentary secretaries earn an extra $10,500 a year.

This, That, and The Other Thing

In this medley of odds and ends we do our best to amaze and tantalize with a miscellany of information that touches on everything from everyday events and Canadian firsts to tiny jails, the family car and a community where the streets really are paved with gold.

So, what are those little balls that move around on the side of gas pumps? Is it possible to get your home into the movies? When did the first station wagon cruise the streets of Canada and how exactly do you get your name into a Canadian who's who book?

Before you make your way through this section, we pose one final question: How did an Ontario man, once known as a "Canadian blowhard," get his picture onto an American postage stamp?

We think the answer will amaze you.

QUESTION?   *Are the streets of Yellowknife in the Northwest Territories paved with gold?*

ANSWER.   Take a stroll along the main drag of the Territorial capital city and you won't exactly trip over gold nuggets but you will be walking atop traces of the precious metal, says Terry Foster, chair in 1997 of the City of Yellowknife Heritage Committee.

That's because some of the streets were originally made with waste from gold mines. "Given that they were never able to extract all the gold, there would be gold in the granular material and pavement … Given that most of our gravel comes from crushed rock, there is likely some gold in all our pavement," says Foster.

So, the local Yellowknife saying, "The streets are paved with gold" is in fact true! But we suspect municipal officials won't be too pleased if you start chipping away at local roadways with a miner's pick.

Foster also points out another interesting fact about Yellowknife's connection to gold. "Another local saying, and one that certainly is correct, is that "the gold is paved with streets." That's because both of Yellowknife's gold mines run beneath the city's streets.

QUESTION?

Where can you watch a play where the stage is in Canada but the audience sits in the United States?

ANSWER.

This unique experience takes place at the Haskell Free Library and Opera House which straddles the Vermont–Quebec border. Officials say it's the only public institution in the world that straddles a border like that.

The library/opera house, which has been featured in "Ripley's Believe it Or Not," was built between 1901 and 1904 and sits in the communities of Derby Line, Vermont, and Rock Island, Quebec. When you walk into the building, you even see a boundary line painted on the floor running through the reading room and the four-hundred-seat opera house. The entrance to the library is in the United States, but the sixteen thousand volumes of books in the stack room are wholly in Canada. And the stage and a few seats of the opera house are in Canada while most of the seats are in America.

A line in the middle of the Haskell Free Library shows the U.S.–Canada border.

[Photo: Catherine Blake]

The building was a gift from Martha Stewart Haskell, a Canadian who had the library/opera house built in honour of her husband Carlos, who was American. The first show in the opera house, which was modelled on the old Boston Opera House, took place in 1904 and featured the Columbian Minstrels. The library/opera house underwent renovations in May 1997 which involved government officials from both Canada and the United States. Apparently, there were a lot of legalities to overcome because of different building code regulations, but the job was completed. At one point an elevator built in Canada had to be lowered in by crane from the Canadian side of the border across the boundary line so that the American crew could install it. Building regulations wouldn't allow it any other way.

The opera house has featured speakers, plays, and concerts for more than ninety years. At one time there were discussions about having the Beatles perform there because one of them was having immigration hassles. The group would have been able to legally perform on the Canadian stage for American audiences. The plans fell through, however.

Although a great deal of co-operation has taken place in maintaining this unique institution, there are still different prices depending on the currency you use. Admission to a 1997 show was eight dollars (US) for adults, but Canadians had to ante up ten dollars.

QUESTION?   *In what province do people drink the most and least amount of beer?*

ANSWER.   You might want to pour yourself a cold one as you read this. According to information from the Brewers Association of Canada, the top beer drinkers in Canada live in the Yukon Territory. Latest statistics (from 1996) show that people there consumed 113.90 litres each on average. That works out to an average of 334 bottles of beer per person for the year.

However, the association doesn't really consider the Yukon to be the leader. The extraordinary high number is attributed to fluctuations in the population due to the influx each summer of a seasonal work force and of tourists, and is therefore not really reflective of the population base, the association notes. It also reports that Quebeckers, who drank 72.86 litres or about 214 bottles of beer per person, rank first.

Next on the list are people from Newfoundland, at 70.74 litres (207 bottles) per person, and British Columbians, at 65.89 litres (193 bottles) per capita. At the bottom of the barrel were people from the Northwest Territories, at 47.53 litres (139 bottles) per person. The Canadian average, by the way, was 65.33 litres (191 bottles), which is well below that of the peak drinking year of 1979, when the average was 85.31 litres or 250 bottles of beer. That still comes nowhere near the intake of drinkers in the Czech Republic who consume 160 litres of beer annually per capita.

For those with a head for figures, bottled beer accounts for 68 per cent of the Canadian market, cans 20 per cent and draught 12 per cent. Bottled beer is the more popular of the three in most areas of the country, with the exception of Alberta, British Columbia, and the Yukon, where drinkers prefer to quaff from cans.

Two other points to ponder when you're picking up a six pack: Canada is the fifth-largest exporter of beer in the world and Canadian beer is the highest taxed in the world, just edging out Norway.

QUESTION?

Why did the Canadian brewing industry switch from tall bottles to "stubbies," then back to tall ones?

ANSWER.

Since the first Canadian beer bottle was produced in 1825 in Mallorytown, Ontario, at Mallorytown Glass Works, the containers that have held Canadian beer have taken many shapes — from tall and chubby, to short and stubby, to tall and slim, as is the case today.

By the way, the first beer bottles were blown by hand. It was not until 1906, at the Diamond Glass Company in Montreal, that the first beer bottle was manufactured on a machine, according to a 1986 article published in the *Canadian Brewerianist*, a newsletter for collectors of beer bottles and memorabilia and for people interested in Canada's brewery industry.

By the early fifties, the number of bottle styles and capacities had gradually been reduced to two main styles and capacities — the twelve-ounce "pint," and the twenty-two-ounce "quart." Both were tall bottles.

In eastern Canada, two pint styles existed. One was known as "ale" and had a long concave sloping shoulder; the other, called "lager," possessed a relatively straight shoulder and neck area which bulged sharply to meet the bottle's body. The quart was basically the same as today's twenty-two-ounce bottle, which is popular in certain areas of the country, including Ottawa, Quebec and the Atlantic provinces. Western Canada used the "lager" style, in brown glass, for virtually all beer products and also employed the same quart bottle we use today.

The switch to more compact bottles, known as "stubbies" or "squats," came in March 1962, after four years of intensive study by the brewing industry which had come to the conclusion that green and clear bottles were too heavy and their shape was inefficient for warehousing.

The stubbies held the same amount of beer but at nine ounces they weighed 25 per cent less than the tall bottles, meaning a case of twenty-four weighed five pounds less than a case of tall bottles. And because the stubbies were three inches shorter, they were easier to store in warehouses. So, the change meant breweries were hauling 185,000 fewer tons of weight per year and getting more cases of beer in each truck, resulting in substantial savings in freight and transportation. In addition, bars could store more beer in less space and the amber-colored bottles protected beer from the sun's harmful ultraviolet rays, while green and clear ones did not.

While most stubbies looked alike, there was one distinct stubby brought out by Carling-O'Keefe. It was a special keg-shaped bottle, generally available only in Ontario and Quebec, and designed to promote Heidelberg Beer.

The era of the stubby was short, however. Although a superior container, it was not chic enough for the 1980s beer drinker. Between 1982 and 1984 the Canadian brewing industry rejected the stubbies and went back to tall bottles because it opted for bottling in distinctive packages, known as "private mold" bottles. The switch to these containers, with new labelling, was an attempt to set one brand apart from the other as a way of increasing market share.

Amstel Breweries in Hamilton, Ontario, was first to receive permission to bottle its beer in a distinct bottle and others soon followed. At one point Canadians were drinking out of at least eight different long-neck bottles. But because of chaos with sorting, breweries eventually went to a standard long neck and the private molds were assigned to different provinces. Newfoundlanders, for example, received their beer for several years in private-mold Carling bottles, reports Loren Newman of Bright's Grove, Ontario, publisher of the *Canadian Brewerianist*.

The industry may have saved money by going to stubbies but the return to tall bottles cost big bucks. The country's three major breweries wrote off a total of $59 million in bottle inventory, spent $120 million buying new glass, paid higher distribution costs because of the different shapes and sizes and spent millions telling Canadians about the change.

And costs remain high, largely because tall bottles don't last as long as the shorter variety. Stubbies were used up to twenty-five times before being discarded; the new ones are used only ten times, partly because twist-off caps damage the delicate threads at the top of the bottle and partly because breweries decided scuffed bottles didn't create a positive image for their products.

If you're wondering what happened to all the bottles that were no longer used each time styles changed, here is the answer: When long necks gave way to stubbies, there were about 300 million bottles to be disposed of. Eventually each of the clear-glass bottles was crushed for re-use in the manufacture of other clear-glass containers. Some of the glass was used in the making of the new amber stubby bottle.

Because of their colour, the millions of green bottles presented a larger problem. Less than 10 per cent of the bottles were sold to overseas markets, including North Africa and South America, for use as beer bottles and to companies in the United States for bottling soft drinks. That left 15.5 million dozen green bottles. A small number were put to novel use in different parts of Canada; a curling rink in the Maritimes, for example, used thousands of the crushed containers for drainage and insulation.

Eventually the brewers bought back the remaining bottles to be used in the production of new glass. No one seems to know how many stubbies were in circulation when the changeover was made to long necks but the Brewers Association of Canada estimates there were more stubbies than long necks.

Many stubbies were crushed and re-used in other glass products, but because there wasn't a huge market for brown glass at the time, plenty of stories circulated about the fate of the stubbies: For example, Labatt's and later Carling-O'Keefe filled them with private-label beer which was shipped to Kentucky in the hope the bottles would never return to Canada. Another tale had the empties sitting in an aircraft hanger somewhere near Toronto. Some were sent to the Caribbean and Europe where they were used as exotic bottles.

"The breweries certainly tried everything, anything they could think of to get rid of those bottles. The line was 'Does anyone want a few bottles cheap?'" says Mr. Newman.

In the early 1990s an industry standard was adopted. Today all Canadian breweries put their beer in the same style bottles.

QUESTION?

How many people are in jail in Canada every day and what does it cost to keep them there?

ANSWER.

An average of 33,800 persons are behind bars in Canada on any given day, indicates a Statistics Canada report by researchers Micheline Reed and Peter Morrison. The latest data available show that about 14,000 of these were inmates in federal penitentiaries in 1995–96 and 19,700 were in provincial/territorial facilities. Another 120,200 offenders were living in the community under supervision rather than behind bars.

We checked back about a decade to see if the numbers of crooks in the clink has increased and the answer is a definite yes. In 1986–87, Statistics Canada reported that 26,673 men and women were in the slammer, with 15,567 inmates in provincial/territorial jails and another 11,106 in federal facilities. Back then, only 80,080 offenders were living in the community under supervision. The typical offender serving a provincial sentence (under two years) was male, aged thirty-one years, convicted of a property offence and serving a one-month sentence. The typical federal offender (sentences of two years or more) was male, aged thirty-three years, convicted of robbery and serving a forty-six-month sentence. Women made up 9 per cent of the people sentenced to provincial/territorial institutions in 1995–96 but just 3 per cent of federal convicts.

Judging by the suicide rate in prisons, life in jail is no cake walk: Statistics Canada notes that ninety-four inmates took their own lives in 1995–96, more than twice the suicide rate of the Canadian adult population living on the outside.

The cost of providing adult correctional services was $1.9 billion in 1995–96, and the average cost of keeping a con behind bars was $42,300 or $115 per day for an offender who spends a year in jail.

QUESTION?   *Do Canadians hold the world record for building the biggest snowman?*

ANSWER.   We did once, but the record was eclipsed by people in Anchorage, Alaska, and has been topped a couple of times since. The most recent record, according to *The Guinness Book of World Records*, was set in 1995 by residents of Yamagata, Japan. Over ten days and nights they built a snowman that was 96 feet 7 inches (about 29.4 metres) high.

It was during Winnipeg's Festival du Voyageur in February 1988 that Canadians built a then-record snowman of 15.6 metres tall (about 51 feet). The reign was brief, however, because the Anchorage snowman was completed in March of the same year and stood 63 1/2 feet tall (about 19.3 metres). This snowman was built despite high winds and temperatures above freezing. The cubes of snow were lifted into place by a crane. Other Alaskans did even better in 1992, building a man from snow that was 76 feet 2 inches (about 23.2 metres), and people in Saas-Fee, Switzerland built one a year later that reached 90 feet 1 inch (or 27.4 metres).

However, as far as we know the Winnipeg snowman still holds the record for the world's largest toque, which was made of 45 kilometres of yarn, was 4.9 metres in diameter, and 4.3 metres long.

QUESTION?

What is the story behind the S.S. Moyie, a sternwheeler docked at Kaslo, British Columbia?

ANSWER.

The S.S. *Moyie*, which for nearly sixty years plied the waters of Kootenay Lake in southeast British Columbia, is the last passenger-carrying sternwheeled steamboat to operate in western North America and is also the oldest surviving intact vessel of her type in the world.

In nearly six decades of service very few changes were made to her cabins, hull or machinery, notes Victoria author Robert D. Turner in a book written in 1991. The *Moyie* was one of hundreds of steam-powered sternwheelers that plied the rivers of western North America after the mid-1800s and into the 1950s, often as the only means of reliable transportation into remote areas. It carried settlers, travellers, miners, tourists and excursion crowds, as well as immigrants seeking

The S.S. *Moyie* at Kaslo, B.C.

[Photo: Randy Ray]

new homes, internees torn from theirs, soldiers going to war and cargo, such as silver and copper, apples, wood, mail, beer and wine, cattle and horses, wagons and automobiles.

It was owned by the Canadian Pacific Railway. The steel frames were built in Toronto at Bertram Engine Works and the boat was assembled in Nelson, British Columbia. The *Moyie* was named after a mining community in southern British Columbia, situated on the almost-completed Crowsnest Past railway line.

It was launched on October 22, 1898, had a passenger capacity of 250 people and was 161.7 feet (48.5 metres) long by 30.1 feet (9 metres) wide. It was retired on August 21, 1958, when highway and air travel became the norm. Her sternwheel is 21.8 feet (6.5 metres) long and 19.4 feet (5.8 metres) wide. She steamed an estimated 2,000 miles (3,200 kilometres) in her years of service and was once described as "an ornament to the lake service of the CPR."

The S.S. *Moyie* is a national historic site and a provincial historic landmark.

QUESTION?

Whatever happened to the alternate name — the Macdonald–Cartier Freeway — for Highway 401 in Ontario?

ANSWER.

The 401, which runs from the Quebec border to Windsor, Ontario, is the spine along which most of the province's growth has taken place in the past forty years. It's been described as "the most important single development changing the social and economic pattern of Ontario." The 401 was still legally known as the MacDonald–Cartier Freeway as of 1997, but it's doubtful you'd find many motorists who would call it that.

The idea for the 401 originated during World War II, when information gathered from a survey of drivers indicated where such a route should be built for ease of travel. Many critics thought the idea of building a highway to bypass Toronto was foolish and that it wouldn't be used. Anyone who is stuck in traffic there today knows how wrong that assumption was. To appreciate just how much things have changed, consider this description of the bypass in 1956: a "motorist's dream," providing "some of the most soothing scenery in the Metropolitan area."

The name of the 401 was changed in 1965 by Ontario's premier John Robarts to honour two of Canada's Fathers of Confederation Sir John A. Macdonald and Sir Georges Étienne Cartier. Signs were placed along the highway indicating the name change, but once the signs got old, they were taken down and never replaced.

John Shragge, who helped edit a history of the highway and who worked for the Ontario Ministry of Transportation for many years, says he has "no idea why the new name never caught on. It was a good name, very Canadian and very historical."

Canadians tend not to name highways after historical figures the way Americans in their patriotic verve do, he observes. "There seems to be a lot of negative feeling about doing it. I don't know why." Although you won't see signs with the full official name on it these days, there are still smaller signs along the 401 that say "M-C Freeway."

Other highways in Ontario, with the exception of the Queen Elizabeth Way or QEW as it's called, have been given names but these generally don't catch on like the numbers do, Shragge explains. For example, Highway 11, which runs from Toronto to the Manitoba border, was called the Ferguson Highway from the 1920s until World War II, but "eventually that usage just fell off and now it's Highway 11." And Highway 2 in Ontario used to be called the Provincial Highway. Numbers for highways became popular in southern Ontario in the 1920s and spread in usage in the 1930s.

QUESTION?   *Which animal is more popular among
Canadian pet owners — dogs or cats?*

ANSWER.   If we go by somewhat dated information from
Statistics Canada, cats are second to dogs by a
whisker. According to figures obtained when
this question was last surveyed in the late
1980s, there were approximately 2,205,000 pet
dogs in Canada compared to 2,044,000 pet
cats. And Statistics Canada informs us that
about 41 per cent of households in Canada owned a pet, a percentage
that has remained constant since the early eighties. The data showed
that 23.3 per cent of households had
at least one dog and 21.6 per cent had
at least one cat.

**They may be man's best
friend, but dogs run second
to cats in popularity.**
[Photo: Catherine Blake]

But more recent figures from a
petfood industry publication suggest
that pet cats have the upper paw on
dogs. A survey of pet populations per
100 humans in 11 European
countries, the United States, Australia,
Canada and Japan showed there were
16 cats per 100 humans in Canada,
compared to 12 dogs per 100 humans.
The U.S. figures showed 25 cats per
100 versus 21 dogs, but the people
responsible for the survey question
the accuracy of those numbers.
Interestingly enough, in Australia, the
Netherlands, Belgium, Luxembourg
and Italy, caged birds are much more
popular pets than either cats or dogs.

Another source, the Canadian
Animal Health Institute, estimated
there were about four million cats in

Canada compared to about three million dogs, and that we spent almost $900 million annually on their care and feeding.

The Canadian Kennel Club claims that Labrador retrievers have been the most popular breed registered in Canada for the past three years, with golden retrievers and German shepherds running second and third. Himalayans have been at the top for more than a decade when it comes to most popular breed of cat in Canada, states the Canadian Cat Association. Persians are second and Siamese are third.

QUESTION?   *Have Canadians ever been commemorated on American postage stamps?*

ANSWER.   Over the years, Americans have licked four stamps issued to pay tribute to people with roots in Canada, according to the United States Postal Service.

The Oregon Territory three-cent stamp issued in 1948 commemorates John McLoughlin, a native of Rivière-du-Loup, Quebec, and Jason Lee, born in Stanstead, Quebec, which at the time was considered a part of Vermont. The stamp features a covered wagon, pulled by a team of horses or mules flanked on the left by a headshot of McLoughlin and on the right by Lee. The words Oregon Territory Centennial are under the wagon, notes U.S. post office spokesman Barry Ziehl.

McLoughlin was an explorer and fur trader, and later a physician, who joined the North West Fur Company, which later merged with the Hudson's Bay Company. In 1824, he was made director of the Hudson's Bay Company, and established a headquarters at Fort Vancouver, now Vancouver, Washington, where he organized new trading posts, kept peace among the Native people and won control of the fur trade on the Pacific coast. Recognizing Oregon's potential, he encouraged settlement of the region by French Canadian farmers. Eventually he resigned from the Hudson's Bay Company and became an American citizen.

Lee was a Methodist clergyman who was recognized as a pioneering missionary in the Pacific Northwest. He set up the Oregon Mission to establish schools and agriculture near Salem, Oregon, and also formed the Oregon Institute, now Willamette University. He later returned to Stanstead, Quebec, where he died in 1845.

Four-cent stamps released in 1959 in the Silver Centennial issue commemorate the one hundredth anniversary of the discovery of silver at Mount Davidson in the Virginia Range, in Nevada. The Canadian involved was Henry T.P. Comstock, who was born in Trenton, Ontario, and in 1859 claimed ownership of a vein rich in gold and silver. The find led to the establishment of Virginia City, which is now a ghost town. The lode yielded more than $300 million in gold and silver in the first twenty years and was abandoned in 1898.

The stamp depicts three prospectors near a trough, including Comstock who laid claim to the land after leaving Canada and working in the fur trade in New Mexico. Comstock, who was nicknamed "old pancake" and is described in one American history book as "a Canadian blowhard," sold his share in the find for $11,000 and later lost his money in a bad investment. Eleven years after striking it rich, he died, either by suicide or at the hands of robbers.

The six-cent Father Marquette stamp was issued in 1968 in honour of Louis Jolliet (spelled Joliet on the U.S. stamp), a French Canadian explorer and Jesuit priest born in Beaupré, near Quebec City, and Jacques Marquette, a French explorer and missionary. The stamp features a canoe with four people in it, one of whom is believed to be Jolliet. He and Marquette sailed the Mississippi River, reaching the mouth of the Arkansas River in mid-July 1673, and ventured far enough south to prove the Mississippi flowed into the Gulf of Mexico, rather than the Pacific Ocean. Jolliet later explored Labrador and Hudson Bay and was appointed royal hydrographer of New France in 1697.

Vilhjalmur Stefansson, a native of Arnes, Manitoba, appears on the twenty-two-cent Arctic Explorer stamp released in 1986. The stamp features the controversial explorer's photograph, an Arctic scene and a map of the Arctic. The son of Icelanders, he moved with his family to the Dakotas in 1880; he explored the Arctic between 1906 and 1918, covering more than thirty-two thousand square kilometres of the frigid territory. His message was that the Arctic was not bleak and frozen wasteland but a habitable region which must be developed.

Stefansson discovered some of the world's last unknown major land masses, including Lougheed, Borden, Meighen and Brock islands but was dogged by controversy after making enemies during the Canadian Arctic expedition between 1913 and 1918 and because some of his projects went bust. One such failure was his plan to domesticate reindeer in northern Canada. After the mid-1920s most of his time was spent in the United States, where he was regarded as one of the world's foremost arctic experts. He died in Hanover, New Hampshire.

Michael Schreiber, spokesman for Linn's Stamp News, an influential publication based in Sidney, Ohio, says the four stamps are "common commemoratives" valued today at between twenty-five and fifty cents each.

QUESTION?   *How did the Kiwanis club get its name and did it start in Canada?*

 ANSWER. The club began in Detroit in 1915, and the first Canadian chapter opened in Hamilton a year later. Kiwanis didn't extend outside those two countries until 1962, when it moved into Mexico. The club was originally called the Benevolent Order of Brothers, indicates a district administrative secretary for Kiwanis, and was established for the mutual granting of preferred treatment in professional and business dealings. The club's founder, Allen Browne, didn't like the name, however, and with the help of a local historian he came up with the name Kiwanis. The spokesperson declares the name comes from the North American Indian phrase "Nun Keewanis," which roughly translates as "to express oneself." Another translation that has been suggested is "We have a good time — we make noise." She says the word was found in a book called *Bishop Baraga's Dictionary of Otchipew.*

The club's purpose was to provide a forum for professional and business dealings, but community service soon became the club's raison d'être. Currently, there are approximately 13,000 members of Kiwanis in Canada. There are more than 319,000 members worldwide in more than 8,600 clubs in 79 nations and geographic areas.

QUESTION?   *I used to rely a lot on Coles Notes when I was in high school. Are they still popular?*

ANSWER.   Hands up if anyone remembers the first Coles Notes booklet written in 1948 was for the French novella *Colomba* by Prosper Mérimée. The book was a requirement for Grade Thirteen students, and the translation of the story from French into everyday English sold well and remained in print for many years. The booklet wasn't called a Coles Note at the time; that came later in the early 1950s.

Spurred by that success, Coles hired a Shakespearean specialist to do a set of student review notes for *The Merchant of Venice*. According to a spokesperson at Coles, the Coles Notes line, which celebrated its fiftieth anniversary in 1998, is still popular with students; sales figures aren't available, however.

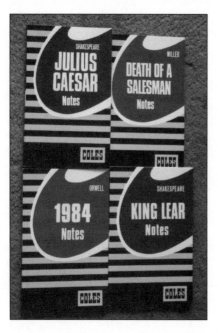

In the late 1980s about 500,000 Coles Notes were sold annually, but sales reached their peak during the time baby boomers were going to high school, in the 1960s and early 1970s.

There are more than 120 titles, with the vast majority of them dealing with English novels and plays. Other subjects include physics, languages, math, and chemistry. Although Coles Notes were considered something of a

Coles Notes have been with us since 1948 and are still going strong.

[Photo: Catherine Blake]

no-no by teachers twenty-five years or more ago, a spokesperson says Coles receives very few complaints about them nowadays. One reason may be that students aren't relying as much on the Notes as their predecessors may have done.

"The kids use it more as a reference source these days [and not as a substitute for the book]. Certainly, any educator would be upset if students relied just on Coles Notes, without reading the book."

In fact, inside the booklets one finds the statement: "Proper use of Coles Notes will allow the student to pay greater attention to lectures and spend less time taking notes." Coles Notes are usually written by experts in their field, who are paid as freelancers.

The Notes are updated periodically, and over the years titles get dropped. Some of the booklets that have been deleted in the past are *Barchester Towers*, *Cider With Rosie*, *Old Testament as Literature*, and *Renaissance Drama*. Jack Cole, the founder of Coles, sold the American rights to the idea and the booklets became the popular Cliff's Notes that are sold in the United States.

Coles Notes have been sold in more than seventy countries. Notes for Shakespearean plays still remain the most popular sellers today, including such titles as *Macbeth*, *Hamlet* (the two best selling titles ever), and *King Lear*. *English Grammar Simplified* and *How to Write Good Essays & Critical Reviews* are also top sellers. The best selling Canadian-literature title is *The Stone Angel* by Margaret Laurence.

Where is Canada's largest tombstone?

ANSWER.

The gravestone in question marks the burial place of Peter Verigin near Brilliant, British Columbia, and it's about the size of a large billboard, Calgary author Nancy Millar writes in her book *Once Upon A Tomb: Stories from Canadian Graveyards*. Verigin, who was a hero to his Doukhobor followers, is buried on a rocky ledge above the Kootenay River and his epitaph is written in Russian and English with white paint on a rock face about ten metres tall.

Verigin's body was originally buried beneath an elaborate Italian-marble monument which was blown up, explains Millar. At that point, his followers placed the body in a concrete bunker that was surrounded by a high chain-link fence topped with barbed wire.

The destruction of the first grave marker was Verigin's second explosion: In 1924 he was killed by a bomb as he travelled by train while trying to keep the peace between Doukhobors and Canadian authorities. Millar says a breakaway Doukhobor sect was suspected in both explosions but nothing was ever proven. Verigin died at age sixty-five.

QUESTION?

How long have station wagons been available in Canada?

ANSWER.

Canadian roadways saw the first wagons in 1912, when they were produced one at a time by custom body shops on chassis purchased from Ford Motor Company. The vehicles were converted Model T's. The first mass-produced station wagon available in Canada was built by Ford in 1929. It was an eight-passenger wagon with a body made of hard maple with birch panelling. Folks who needed the room, either for work, pleasure, or to haul their families around, could pick one up for $890 in Canada or $695 in the United States, says Ford of Canada historian Sandra Notarianni of Oakville.

The 1929 Ford, Canada's first mass-produced station wagon.
[Photo: Courtesy of Ford of Canada Archives]

The wagon could be used either as a passenger-carrying car or a delivery unit. Extra luggage space could be created by lowering the tailgate to support bags or trunks, or by removing seats in the rear compartment. The wagon's seats were cobra, cross-grained, black artificial leather and interior trim was black. It had windows made from heavy celluloid.

Close to 5,000 wagons were produced the first year, all in Michigan. They could reach speeds of up to sixty miles per hour. *Ford News*, the company newspaper, called the wagon "a most valuable addition to the motor vehicle equipment of country clubs and estates because of its high utility value. Added to this is good appearance."

In August 1997 the value of a 1929 station wagon in fully restored condition was about $18,000 (U.S.). Notarianni points out that many are still in existence today, mostly in the hands of collectors and in classic-car museums.

Tony Durham, director of the Automation Evolution Centre in Kingston, Ontario, tells us that station wagons were developed in North America because people wanted larger vehicles to transport visitors and luggage between train stations and their homes and also for hunters — usually wealthy people with large estates — who used them to haul dogs, guns and game.

It was not until the late 1940s that the station wagon caught on as a family car. In 1948, Ford increased wagon production to 10,312 units to meet the increasing demand. By the early 1960s total auto-industry production exceeded one million wagons, but in the early 1980s production tailed off as the minivan gained popularity.

QUESTION?

Do those little balls that move around on the side of gasoline pumps when you fill up have any purpose?

ANSWER.

Not really. Those balls, usually marbles but sometimes shaped like paddle wheels, are located in what is known as the visible flow indicator or sight glass. According to a spokesperson from a manufacturer in the gasoline pumps industry, the indicators were there to show that gasoline (the liquid in the glass) was flowing through the pumps and that there were no air bubbles present.

However, as of the late 1980s, the federal government no longer required the indicators, because they didn't serve any real purpose. You don't need the indicator to know that gas is being pumped into the car.

The Pump Manufacturers Association had been asking the government for years to drop this requirement and the government complied. Canada was one of the last countries in the world to use them, and for the most part they are now a thing of the past here as well, the spokesperson added.

Those little balls at the side of gas pumps are there for show more than anything else these days.

[Photo: Catherine Blake]

QUESTION?   *I've heard Canada is home to the world's largest dump truck. True?*

ANSWER.   The truck you speak of is known as the Terex Titan and it's found in Sparwood, British Columbia, a coal-mining town of about four thousand people situated at the eastern entrance to British Columbia through the Crowsnest Pass. Once used by the Elkview Coal Corporation, the truck now sits next to Sparwood's business and visitor information centre and is one of the community's main tourist attractions.

It was manufactured by General Motors of Canada and was brought to Sparwood from California in 1978 to be used in the coal mines. It was retired in 1990, when its operation was no longer cost efficient. In 1994 it was donated to the Sparwood Chamber of Commerce, which refurbished it for display purposes with help from the District of

The world's biggest dump truck at Sparwood, B.C.

[Photo: Janis Ray]

Sparwood, the British Columbia government and private donations.

As trucks go, it's a giant. It is 25 feet 7 inches (about 7.6 metres) wide and 66 feet (19.8 metres) long, weighs 260 tons and can hold a load of 350 tons. The box is big enough to hold two Greyhound buses and two pickup trucks, or two million golf balls. The cab where the driver once sat is 13 feet (3.9 metres) from the ground, and when the box is lifted, the truck is 56 feet (16.8 metres) high. Its tires are 11 feet (3.3 metres) in diameter and each one weighs 4 tons. Total cost of its ten tires was $300,000. The truck's fuel tank holds 800 imperial gallons (3,600 litres) of fuel.

The Titan arrived in Sparwood by train on eight flat cars and was reassembled before being driven to the mine site. It was powered by a 16-cylinder, 3,300-horsepower locomotive engine and its generator was powerful enough to supply power to 250 homes.

QUESTION?   *Can Canada boast the world's longest bar?*

ANSWER.   We could have given you a yard of ale for being correct in the 1980s, but unfortunately this claim to fame is no longer true. The world's longest permanent bar used to be the 340-foot (103.6-metre) long bar in Lulu's Roadhouse in Kitchener, Ontario, and was so acknowledged by *The Guinness Book of Records*. But the bar was cut in half in the early 1990s mostly to improve traffic flow, says Mark Gross, special-events co-ordinator at Lulu's. And as far as he knows there are no plans to try to get back into the record books again.

Lulu's opened in April 1984, at the site of a former department store and it specialized in acts from the fifties, sixties, and seventies. It gained an international reputation because of its long bar and because it fed into baby boomer nostalgia. But not only has the bar changed, so have the kinds of music being played. Lulu's still has oldies acts such as Jerry Lee Lewis, but also features more contemporary bands, country music, and trade shows. The roadhouse holds three thousand people and has about eight bars scattered throughout.

The longest permanent bar, according to the latest edition of *The Guinness Book* is a 405 foot 10 inch counter at South Bass Island, Ohio. But it would need to grow substantially to match what is believed to be the longest bar that ever existed. In its heyday, several decades ago, the bar in Erickson's in Portland, Oregon, ran completely around the saloon stretching for 684 feet (about 208.5 metres).

QUESTION?   *How can Canadians get their homes into the movies?*

ANSWER.   Producers, directors, actors and actresses from both Canada and Hollywood are interested in Canadian homes for two reasons — as sets for movies, TV shows and commercials and as temporary residences for stars making movies in Canada. So, your home could have a starring role.

Foreign and Canadian film companies spend more than $1 billion making more than two hundred movies and TV shows every year in Canada, primarily in British Columbia and Ontario, which are the most popular venues in Hollywood North. Among TV shows shot in Canada, up to 1998, are "The X-Files," "The Outer Limits," "Beasties" and "Reboot," all in British Columbia; "Lost Daughters and Painted Angels" in Saskatchewan, and in Ontario, "Goosebumps," "Traders" and "Due South." Movies made in Canada include *Fly Away Home*, *To Die For*, *The Long Kiss Goodnight* (Toronto) and *Legends of the Fall* (Vancouver).

If you feel your home has movie-set potential, send a series of photographs featuring panoramic views of both the inside and outside to the Ontario Film Development Corporation in Toronto or the British Columbia Film Commission in Vancouver. They'll set up a file that is screened on a regular basis by location scouts and movie producers who are looking for the perfect setting for movies, TV shows and commercials. In Saskatchewan there is no official registry of homes, but Sask Film and Video Development Corporation has a photo library of "character" homes, spokesman Murray Messaros points out, and homeowners are welcome to submit photographs.

In other provinces where registries aren't kept, you'll have to hope your home catches the eye of a scout looking for just the right set. And it does happen: In the mid-1990s, the outside of a home in Chester, Nova Scotia, was used to film parts of the movie *Dolores Claiborne*, based on a book by author Stephen King.

To make it onto the silver screen, your home will likely need unique characteristics, such as the long, tree-lined driveway, ivy-covered exterior walls and European château-style design that attracted motion pictures *Legends of the Fall* and *The Fly II* to the Langley, British Columbia, home of Rebecca Black. Black's home has been used as a set for a number of other movies and several TV shows.

But there's also a place for run-of-the-mill bungalows, explains a spokesman for the Toronto Film and Television Office. A small family home in west Toronto, for instance, had a part in the 1994 movie *To Die For*, with Nicole Kidman, because its nondescript decor fit the script. Homes with older kitchens are also in demand for movies set in the 1950s, says a Toronto location scout.

If your home doesn't have set potential, you can rent it out as a home away from home for performers, producers and directors while they're filming in Canada. Stars who have rented places in Toronto include Tom Cruise, Shirley MacLaine and Diane Keaton. In both Toronto and Vancouver, property management companies cater to the stars. One, for instance, found MacLaine a three-bedroom home in Toronto's posh Forest Hill area, where she lived during the shooting of *Mrs. Winterbourne*.

If your home is used for a set, you could earn more than $1,000 a day, for up to thirty days, or your place could be prissied up, at no cost to you, to set the scene for a movie. It's up to the homeowner to negotiate the best deal. One Toronto family had a $5,000 patio installed to set the stage for a scene shot in their backyard. Of course, the patio was theirs to keep. And you may get to meet the stars: While *Legends of the Fall* was being filmed at Black's home, she and her daughter got to hang out with Hollywood hunk Brad Pitt.

If you rent to a star, your one-bedroom apartment could reap more than $3,000 a month, while a home in a posh area like Toronto's Rosedale could fetch between $7,000 and $30,000 a month. But don't sit by the telephone awaiting a call from Steven Spielberg. In Ontario and British Columbia, fewer than 10 per cent of the more than 2,000 homes in location registries make it to the screen. And like many a budding star, your place may end up on the cutting room floor: Scenes shot at Black's home were edited out of the movie. Oh well, she and her daughter still have memories of lounging with Pitt.

QUESTION?   *What can you tell me about the first patent filed in Canada? How is patent protection obtained?*

ANSWER.   The first patent submitted in what was to become Canada was filed by inventor Noah Cushing for a "washing and fulling" machine on June 8, 1824. It was filed in Quebec City in Lower Canada, under British patent law.

The laws of the day gave Cushing's washing machine fourteen years of protection in Upper and Lower Canada, according to Peter Dupuis, information officer, Canadian Intellectual Property Office. Documents filed with the patent office described the invention as having "Two pendulums suspended from the uprights, at the extremity of each of which is a block — one is loaded for washing, the other is grooved, which pendulums are worked and set in motion by a handle which is affixed to two arms, which are attached to the pendulums."

The first Canadian patent granted to a female inventor, also before the country became Canada, was to Ruth Adams for a "reverse cooking stove," in 1855, also under British patent law.

The first patent after Confederation was applied for by William Hamilton of Toronto on July 30, 1869, and was granted on August 18, 1869, under The Patent Act of the Dominion of Canada. Hamilton's invention was a machine for measuring liquids, known in diagrams obtained from the patent office as "Hamiltons Eureka Fluid Meter." Under the Canadian act, the device was given five years of patent protection.

Patents are granted by the federal government to give inventors exclusive rights to produce their inventions for a twenty-year period. Each year, about 110 patent examiners — men and women with an engineering background — determine which of about twenty-five thousand applications should be accorded patents.

Recent patents granted through the Canadian Intellectual Property Office in Hull, Quebec, include: an illuminating brick, a toilet-seat structure capable of automatically feeding seat-covering paper onto a toilet seat; a light-weight anchor; a vandal-proof pay-telephone handset and a child-proof measuring cup.

Dupuis says it takes the average Canadian inventor up to four years to receive a patent. Statistics Canada indicates that Canadian inventors spend close to two years working on an invention before applying for protection. Statscan also reports that a study of inventors between 1978 and 1983 reveals that 99 per cent of inventors are male; forty-six is the median age for Canadian inventors and an inventor's average education is thirteen and a half years.

If you have invented something you feel is worth protecting with a patent, you can obtain further information by contacting Industry Canada, Canadian Intellectual Property Office, 50 Victoria Street, Place du Portage, Phase I, Hull, Quebec K1A 0C9.

QUESTION? *Some art history books say the Group of Seven consisted of as many as ten Canadian painters. Who were the original seven and who joined later?*

ANSWER. Known primarily for landscape paintings characterized by broad brushstrokes and bold colours, the original Group of Seven was made up of A. Y. Jackson, Lawren Harris, Frank Carmichael, Franz Johnston, Arthur Lismer, J. E. H. MacDonald and F. H. Varley.

Members befriended each other in Toronto between 1911 and 1913, and all except Harris, who was independently wealthy, earned their living as commercial artists. The group's first show was in Toronto in 1920.

Johnston left the group in 1926 and was replaced by A. J. Casson. Wishing to spread its appeal beyond Toronto and the northern Ontario bush which appeared in many of its works, the group admitted Montreal painter Edwin Holgate in 1930 and Winnipeg artist L. L. Fitzgerald in 1932. The Group of Seven disbanded in 1933.

Although many believe Tom Thomson was a member (he was a close friend and inspiration of group members), his 1917 drowning death preceded the group's founding by three years.

QUESTION? *What is the narrowest building in Canada?*

ANSWER.

Exploring Vancouver 2, a guide to the city and its buildings, quotes "Ripley's Believe It Or Not" as claiming that the narrowest building in the world — and therefore Canada — is located on Pender Street in Vancouver.

The building has a depth of 4 feet 11 inches (about 1.5 metres) and runs 96 feet (29.26 metres) along the street. It was built out of spite by prominent businessman Sam Kee, says the book, written by Harold Kalman. In late 1997 it housed an insurance sales office.

The guidebook explains that the city had expropriated most of Kee's property to widen Pender Street but refused to compensate him for a narrow remaining strip of land. Kee's neighbour, in turn, expected to get the strategic corner property very cheaply.

Kee responded by erecting the narrow two-storey building in 1913, using bay windows to add extra space. Its basement, which once contained communal baths, extends well under the street.

The late Bill Birmingham, a Vancouver architect who was co-owner of the building from 1966 until the early 1980s, said the structure was odd enough to attract the attention of the "Ripley's Believe It Or Not" television show several years ago, when his architectural firm occupied its second floor.

"It was a lot of fun. We couldn't have any fat employees, they couldn't get by one another," he quipped.

QUESTION?   *Is it true the Bloody Caesar cocktail is a Canadian drink?*

ANSWER.   Yes, the next time you're downing the Clamato-and-vodka drink you might want to toast the late Walter Chell. The man from Montenegro, who emigrated to Canada in the late 1950s, invented what has been described as Canada's national cocktail, the Bloody Caesar.

Chell was working for the Westin chain of hotels in Calgary when he came up with his now-famous drink in 1969. Legend has it he spent about three months perfecting the cocktail. The drink calls for one ounce of vodka over ice, four ounces of Clamato juice, a dash of Worcester sauce, salt and pepper, all garnished with a celery stalk. Chell had a reputation as a troubleshooter for the hotel chain and his knowledge of food and drink made him a valued employee.

Chell first made the drink by combining juice from his own mashed clams with tomato juice. A source says the drink was originally just called a Caesar, but that changed when an Englishman tasting the drink described it as "a damned good bloody Caesar." Apparently, Mott, the company that later patented canned clamato juice, had a dispute with Chell over the drink, but eventually he was hired as consultant and did endorsements for the company.

Chell got his start in the hotel business in Switzerland and worked in the kitchen of the Aga Khan before moving to Canada. He worked in South Africa for most of the 1970s but returned to Canada, where he worked at the Hotel Toronto. He retired in 1990 and died in 1997.

QUESTION?   *How do you get your name in Canada's various who's who books?*

ANSWER.

There are two main Canadian who's who publications, but you'll have to do something pretty substantial to get into either of them.

The book with the most entries is *Canadian Who's Who*, published by the University of Toronto Press in Toronto. It has been published since 1910, contains about fifteen thousand names and is updated once a year.

Editor Elizabeth Lumley says you must be at the top of your profession or sphere of influence to make it into this book. That can be as president of a major Canadian company, as the leader of a volunteer organization, or as a notable figure in sports, the arts, science or space travel, to name a few of the categories covered. "The book includes a whole range of people, not all of whom are household names but who have been recognized nationally," adds Lumley, who notes that you don't have to be a Canadian to get into the book. Foreign diplomats, visiting scholars or presidents of Canadian companies can be included.

Entries in the *Canadian Who's Who* include all federal and provincial Cabinet ministers, outstanding sports figures like Donovan Bailey, Silken Laumann and Wayne Gretzky, presidents of major companies, including George Cohon of McDonalds of Canada, authors Mordecai Richler and Carol Shields and astronauts Roberta Bondar and Marc Garneau. Don't expect to recognize every name in the book, though. Some are not widely known.

Names are recommended annually by a special board and about twelve hundred new ones are added each year. It is a reference book used by libraries, students and executive search firms who are profiling potential hirees. Since the fall of 1997 it has also been available on CD ROM.

The other major Canadian book of important personalities is *Who's Who In Canada* published by Global Press, a division of Macmillan Canada in Toronto. It has been published since 1909, contains about a thousand names and leans heavily toward business and government people, although literary figures, artists and others are also in the book. It's updated every February.

Global Press publishing director Susan Ritcey says business types generally make it into the book if they've reached the position of president, chief executive officer, or chief financial officer in successful companies. Canadian leaders of professions and governments are also welcomed into the book.

While the amount of money a company makes often corresponds to the success of that company, candidates for *Who's Who In Canada* are not judged on earnings alone. Individual accomplishments such as winning awards, directorship appointments and contributions to their communities represent some of the many attributes that complete the picture of a leader. You don't have to be a Canadian citizen to qualify: Some of those in the book are Americans who run Canadian companies.

But exemplary accomplishments alone won't get you into the *Who's Who In Canada*. Prospective entrants pay $175 for an English listing and $275 for a listing in English and French. For their money, they receive a comprehensive profile, accompanied by a photograph, plus a personal copy of the book.

Ritcey cautions that people can't buy their way into her company's book. All listing submissions are evaluated by an internal advisory committee with a few candidates being turned down every year.

Among those listed in the 1997 version were: Author Margaret Atwood, Prime Minister Jean Chrétien; Frank Stronach, head of Magna International Incorporated, an automobile parts maker; media magnates Conrad Black and Ken Thomson; Claude Lajeunesse, president and vice-chancellor of Ryerson Polytechnic University and Sonia Bata, a director of Canadian shoe company Bata Limited.

QUESTION?

Where is the smallest jail in North America?

ANSWER.

The jail in Rodney, Ontario, is considered to be the continent's tiniest tank. The local tourist commission re-opened the jail in 1995 as a tourist attraction after it had been closed for more than fifty years. The jail, which measures 24.3 square metres (about 270 square feet), has only two tiny cells inside it but is billed as the oldest, smallest jail in North America.

The jail was built in 1890 and is therefore the oldest of its size on the continent, according to Rodney tourist officials. However, when they re-opened the jail with that billing, they were almost immediately challenged by other towns and cities.

Port Dalhousie, near St. Catharines, Ontario, claimed its jail was older by about forty-five years. Historians in Coboconk, Ontario, 150 kilometres northeast of Toronto, also contested Rodney's claim to the title of smallest jail. And, finally, the people of Tweed, Ontario, believed they had the smallest jail as well.

But the people in Rodney stuck by their claim to fame because their building is more of a jail than the one in Port Dalhousie. The structure there was only one room and needed restoration. Tweed eventually admitted Rodney had them beat because its jail, first opened in 1898, measured 4.9 by 6.1 metres (29.89 square metres or about 320 square feet).

QUESTION?   *Why was whiskey called "fire water" in the early days of the Canadian West?*

ANSWER. In the 1860s, when American traders used to exchange alcohol for furs and buffalo hides, pure alcohol was mixed with other ingredients at trading posts to produce a greater volume and, thus, more profit. The watered-down "trade" whiskey used on the frontier was usually made by combining a gallon of raw alcohol with three gallons of water. To this was added a pound of tea, black chewing tobacco, ginger and red peppers.

"The Indians quite correctly referred to it as fire water," notes author D. Bruce Sealey. "The effect of this vile concoction was the same on both Europeans and Indians." Here's how American artist Charles M. Russell described alcohol's effects: "I never knowed what made an Injun so crazy when he drank till I tried this booze … it sure was a brave-maker and if a hand had enough of this booze you couldn't drown him. You could even shoot a man through the brain or heart and he wouldn't die till he sobered up."

The evils of fire water would often surface while Native people were trading for it: Small wonder, when you consider that drinking the booze was part of the trading process. When Native people arrived at the numerous "whiskey posts" that sprang up across Southern Alberta, a standard routine was followed, according to Sealey. Chiefs were invited into the heavily guarded forts and given free liquor; then, after two or three drinks, they left the forts to assemble their people outside the main gate. A small wicket or window in the gate was opened and trading began under the watchful eye of armed men.

The Native people would push their furs, hides and pemmican through the wicket and for each hide would receive a cup of whiskey which had to be downed immediately. This usually led to drunkenness, and eventually horses, guns and sometimes wives and daughters were sold to get more whiskey. Within a couple of hours the traders had everything the Native inhabitants owned. Vicious brawls would often break out among the Native people: men were stabbed, women and children were beaten and if other tribes were present fierce battles sometimes erupted.

Native people also fought with the traders. But this behaviour wasn't limited to Natives — there was an equal amount of violence among the traders who were cooped up in isolated forts, nervous and on edge from the constant fear of attack. Personal disputes often led to violence and murder.

In 1873, the Canadian government had had enough. It formed the North West Mounted Police, largely because wars and massacres were becoming more frequent and debauchery was getting out of control in Canada's West, much of this being caused by fire water.

QUESTION?

Where was Canada's first zoo?

ANSWER.

The first zoo in Canada — and the first in North America, for that matter — was opened near Halifax in 1847 by Andrew Downs, a world-famous naturalist and taxidermist.

His modest five-acre zoo was in operation for twelve years before the first American zoo was founded in Philadelphia. Downs eventually expanded his spread to one hundred acres, and its bears, beaver, mink and elk became a favourite attraction for Halifax residents, who flocked to the site on steamboats. Many of his animals lived in fenced-in enclosures rather than cages.

In 1868, Downs was offered the post of superintendent of New York's Central Park Zoo. He sold his Nova Scotia operation and moved to New York but later turned down the appointment. He returned to Halifax and founded a second zoo, which he sold after experiencing financial trouble.

Mark Kearney was born in Toronto, grew up in Pickering, Ontario, and graduated in journalism from the University of Western Ontario in 1977. Kearney has been a full-time freelance writer since 1989 after working as a reporter for the *London Free Press* and in public relations for the Ontario government. Kearney's articles have appeared in some sixty publications in North America, and he teaches writing at the University of Western Ontario and Lambton College. He is married and lives in London, Ontario.

Randy Ray was born and raised in Toronto and is a graduate of the University of Toronto and Ryerson Polytechnic University. He has been a freelance writer since 1989 after working as a reporter for the *London Free Press* for thirteen years, including three years as the newspaper's Parliament Hill bureau chief. Ray's articles have appeared in more than fifty publications, including *The Ottawa Citizen* and *The Globe and Mail*. He is married, has three children, and lives in Ottawa, Ontario.

Also available

The Great Canadian Trivia Book

THE GREAT CANADIAN TRIVIA BOOK

A Collection of Compelling Curiosities
from Alouette to Zed

Mark Kearney & Randy Ray

by Mark Kearney
and Randy Ray

"A no-fail entertainment and resource ... Kearney and Ray's work deserves to become a classic of the trivia crowd."
— Neil Walker, Editor, *Education Forum*

"Unlike many trivia collections, this one provides plenty of details."
— Jim Robb, *The Ottawa Citizen*

"A veritable resource library of tantalizing tidbits of historical information and other things Canadian."
— Pat Moauro, *The Reporter*

"This book should be a part of the school curriculum. It's a fun way to learn about Canada and learn about our history. It's fantastic."
— Ann Rohmer, CITY-TV/Pulse 24